ALL
ABOUT
JEWELRY

ALL ABOUT JEWELRY

The One Indispensable Guide for Jewelry Buyers, Wearers, Lovers and Investors

BY Rose Leiman Goldemberg

ARBOR HOUSE  *New York*

Library of Congress Catalogue Card Number: 82-72057

ISBN: 0-87795-453-3
Hardcover edition: 0-87795-419-6

Manufactured in the United States of America

10   9   8   7   6   5   4   3   2

This book is printed on acid free paper. The paper in this book meets the guidelines for permanence and durability of the Committee on Production Guidelines for Book Longevity of the Council on Library Resources.

To Bob, Lee and Lisa:
MY REAL JEWELS

Acknowledgments

How can one adequately thank all of the people whose help and encouragement made this book possible?

In the years that I have loved and studied jewelry, I have had the pleasure of learning about it and enjoying it in the best of company. Mrs. Nadia Shepard of Old Mine Road Antiques (Warwarsing, New York) has often been my companion in the contemplation of beautiful old jewelry. Mr. Ward Landrigan of E. J. Landrigan, Inc. (New York City), whose awesome knowledge and affection for colored stones has made him a foremost expert in the field, has shared both generously with me. Mr. Angelo Poliseno, chief goldsmith for designer Jean Schlumberger, whose fabulous jewelry occupies its own suite at Tiffany & Co., has been my friend and teacher. Mr. Anton Marsh, artist and expert in all things old and beautiful, has guided me in the art work for this book. And my friend and agent, Ms. Susan Breitner, whose love of jewelry rivals my own, and who spurred me on to write about it, has often accompanied me in its pursuit.

For the beautiful color photographs and master goldsmith's drawings I am indebted to Ms. Mary Murphy of Christie's, Ms. Vicky Martin of Tiffany & Co., Mr. R. Choly, Mr. Klaus Wisskirchen of Platinum Customcraft Corporation (New York City) and to Mr. Robert Crowningshield of the Gemological Institute of America.

Most of all, I owe thanks to my patient and loving family, my husband Robert L. Goldemberg and my children, Lee and Lisa Schiller.

This book, as all my work, is dedicated to them.

—Rose Leiman Goldemberg
August 1982

Contents

The Lure of Jewelry

Since the beginning of time, men and women have adorned themselves with bright bits of shell or coral, glistening shards of metal, shiny nuggets of stone. Why, when faced with the hardships of survival, did people take the time to smooth and polish and drill and hammer these materials into jewelry? And how did cultures miles and centuries apart find the same objects beautiful, the same colors fascinating, the same shapes and symbols meaningful?

In jewelry store windows, gold, silver, coral, ivory, mother of pearl, rubies, emeralds, turquoise, amethysts, sapphires and diamonds vie for our attention. Whether they are circles, ovals, squares, whorls, rings, beads, bracelets, earrings, snakes, leaves, hands, frogs or stars, the jewels are formed of the same symbols and materials that our ancestors loved and worshiped. How amazing that through all the vagaries of fashion, the parade of styles, the new technologies, we still respond to the same kinds of jewelry. As our ancestors did, we see in them magic, beauty, personal adornment, pleasure and wealth. We appreciate, cherish, protect and pass on our jewelry. It is the most personal of objects, a gift of love. No one forces us to wear it; it is a part of our identity, something we choose for ourselves. Unlike clothes, which we wear out and discard, jewelry is expected to give pleasure for a long time. In buying, wearing and giving jewelry we are participating in a rite as old as humanity itself.

Yet most of us know very little about jewelry, except what our jeweler chooses to tell us. Surely our pleasure in owning and giving jewelry would be enhanced by knowledge. And practically speaking, since fine jewelry is expensive, it is important to learn how to get the best value for your money: what the different gold and silver marks mean, how to tell real pearls and stones from false ones, what gemstones are supposed to look like, how to tell the good from the bad. And, perhaps most important of all, when you own a piece of jewelry you love and cherish, how you can care for and protect it so that it will continue to grow in beauty and value.

I hope this book will introduce you to the pleasure of owning and giving fine jewelry, answer all the questions you can think of—as well as some that might never have occurred to you—about the buying, owning and care of fine jewelry. And give you the security of knowing for sure that what you *do* buy and own is tasteful, genuine and represents good and lasting value.

Gold

Of all the substances of which jewelry is made, perhaps none has a more fascinating history and mystique than gold. The most malleable of the metals, gold is also, as far as we know, the first to have been used in jewelry. It is formed naturally in the earth in a quartzlike rock, and if the deposit is rich enough, the veins of gold can be seen gleaming in the quartz matrix. Because gold is so heavy, when the rocks deteriorate and the gold is washed out, it lies in clumps or nuggets in the bottoms of rivers and streams, and can actually be "panned" out with fine sieves.

Like the rich yellow of the sun, the color of gold has been prized since ancient times, and its virtual indestructibility—1,000-year-old gold vessels and jewelry excavated by archeologists still look as bright and perfect as the day they were made—makes it a natural for fine jewelry. Its relative rarity adds to its worth, and over the years it has been a valuable material on its own and a substitute for money around the world.

One of gold's attributes, however, can also be a shortcoming when it is used for jewelry: it is so soft and malleable that any object made of pure gold will easily bend, scratch and break. Gemstones set in pure gold are easy to lose, because the settings are too soft to hold the stone securely. So gold must be *alloyed* with harder metals, such as silver, copper, nickel, iron or palladium, to bring it to a toughness that will make it strong enough to last. Alloying also affects the gold's color. When mixed with copper it forms pink (red) gold; with silver or cadmium it forms green gold; with nickel, palladium or platinum (or a high proportion of silver), it becomes white gold.

Pure, fine or unalloyed gold is said to be *24-karat* (in England the spelling is "*carat*"). This pure gold doesn't exist naturally, and can only be smelted out of gold ore or nuggets by burning off the small percentage of impurities unavoidable in any product of nature. Twenty-four-karat gold is much too soft to make into objects. It can be bent and molded with the hands, and scratched with a fingernail. Therefore all gold objects contain less than 24 karats of gold.

In choosing gold jewelry, it is important to pick not only the color that is most becoming (and that matches any other pieces you might plan to wear in combination with it), but to choose the karat of gold that is most appropriate for beauty, value and long wear. For example, 22-karat gold, which is rarely seen outside the Orient, is much too soft to wear as a ring or bracelet without danger of denting.

Eighteen-karat gold (which is 75 percent gold and 25 percent alloy) is often used in wedding rings, and, though soft, is beautifully mellow-looking and wears to a satiny patina which grows more and more lovely with the years. It also, alas, becomes thinner and thinner, and very often 18-karat wedding rings eventually break or wear through. Fourteen-karat (fourteen parts of gold to ten of alloy) is tougher and lasts much longer, and is really a better bet for rings, bracelets, brooch backs, spring rings, chains and any parts of jewelry that get sustained hard wear. By the time you get down to 10-karat (popular for baby rings and jewelry, which often has to stand the test of teething), there is more alloy present than gold, and the color and texture are brassy, hard and not so beautiful. However, many lovely pieces are made in these low karats (9- and 12-carat are common in English pieces), and they are not to be dismissed. In America, fourteen is the most common karat, and the majority of pieces are marked 14K. What most of us don't know is that there is a certain amount of leeway accepted in the alloying of gold, so a piece marked 14K may actually contain as little as 13½ karats of pure gold.

There is, of course, a price difference between 18- and 14-karat gold, and you should expect to spend more for high-karat jewelry. Oddly enough, this price differential does not relate too closely to the actual gold content involved, unless the piece is being sold *by weight*, which, though it seems a crude way to handle fine jewelry, is becoming more common in the face of wildly fluctuating gold prices, which make fair pricing difficult. I have seen jewelers in elegant stores slap a beautiful chain or necklace on a gold scale before even quoting price (for selling, not buying). In fact, in times when the gold market is more stable, fine workmanship influences price as much as or more than the gold content, and since 18-karat gold is more easily worked, and therefore is used on pieces which involve more intricate hand workmanship, higher karat pieces tend to be more expensive.

Half of the world's gold is now being mined in South Africa. But there are other countries with gold in sufficient quantity to be commercially useful: Russia, Australia, Alaska, the United States, Canada, Central and West Africa and parts of Europe. Many of the new pieces of jewelry you buy have been melted down from old gold. Truly, gold never dies. Throughout history it has been used over and over, with surprisingly little lost. Your gold wedding ring may have been part of the lives of many other lovers. Perhaps this too is part of our endless fascination for this metal.

The earliest gold ornaments were hammered out of the nearly pure gold found in Egypt and Mesopotamia four centuries before Christ was born. The flat gold sheets were decorated with patterns that were either hammered in with stamps, molded around a piece of wood or metal or incised or engraved with sharp tools. Sometimes a combination of all of these techniques was used.

In ancient Greece, goldwork was raised to an art form involving beautiful *granulation* (tiny balls of gold soldered to the surface of the piece to give a "bloom"), *filigree work* (twisting and weaving of fine wire into patterns), fanciful sculptures in hollow gold, and deeply set stones. During the ensuing centuries, more sophisticated methods of mining, smelting and working gold were discovered, and gold coins became the standard measure of wealth. By the time Columbus sailed for the New World, gold was so important that its discovery in the jungles of Mexico and Central and South America drew explorers and adventurers from all over the civilized world. In Mexico, Cortez gathered up all of the beautifully worked treasures the Indians had created and sent them home to Spain to be melted down. In Peru, Pizarro kidnapped the Inca chief Atahualpa and demanded as ransom a roomful of gold. English pirates preyed on the Spanish galleons full of gold from the New World and managed to win some of it, but most of the melted-down treasures made their way to the coffers of the king of Spain, who became the richest ruler in the world.

The huge new reserves of South and Central American gold were enriched when new sources were discovered in Russia in the eighteenth century. Then, in 1848, gold was discovered in Sutter's Creek, California. Soon after, there were new strikes in Colorado, Montana and Nevada, and

14

the American gold rush was on. And since then our country's love affair with gold has lived on.

In the last decade, the wild fluctuations in the price of gold, reflecting the world's unease and distrust of other forms of wealth, has inflated the price of gold—and therefore gold jewelry—to heights which seem unreasonable. And yet, despite these escalating prices, the sales records of Tiffany, Cartier and Bulgari have never been better. All over the world, people seem to trust the value of this rare and ancient metal more than they trust dollars, yen, pounds or francs. This is what "as good as gold" is all about.

In many countries, gold cannot be sold unless it is marked, and the penalty for mismarking gold is a very steep one. In France, for example, all gold is understood to mean 18-karat gold, and the French gold mark, which looks like a tiny falcon's head, is equivalent to marking a piece 18-karat. The penalty for selling as gold any piece of jewelry that is of lesser quality is imprisonment and loss of license. In the United States, all gold pieces that are made for general sale must be marked with their karat value, and that marking must be correct within half a karat. In England, the most popular carat values are 18, 15 and 12, and other gold marks are used to indicate the city in which the piece was made and the year of manufacture, as well as, sometimes, the jewelry firm that made it. (In this country, too, many makers add their mark; a Tiffany or Cartier piece always bears a special mark, and many other makers consider it a matter of pride to add their name or special sign to those already required by law.)

But all is not gold that glitters. *Gold-filled* or *rolled gold* jewelry, made of a "sandwich" in which base metal (brass, copper or an alloy) is covered on both sides by sheets of gold, is hard to distinguish from the real thing. If the gold is thick enough, the piece will wear well and look like real gold, except that in places where hard wear has rubbed the outer gold off, where the base metal will be visible.

15

The gold that is used can be of various karats, and should be marked accordingly, and the thickness of the gold should be marked too (i.e., ⅟₂₀ or ⅟₁₀). Much less desirable than rolled gold—and much less durable—is *gold plating*, which simply means that a base metal has been electroplated, usually with a very thin coating of gold that rubs off after a few wearings. Gold plating is unsuitable for fine jewelry and should be avoided. Underneath the gold there is usually brass, whence comes the old complaint, "Take off your ring—my finger's turning green!" The ring in question was probably gold plated.

Not all gold jewelry is *solid gold* either. Many pieces are hollow, which of itself is not necessarily bad. But hollow pieces are light and delicate, and often harder to repair than those that are truly solid gold.

So when purchasing any gold jewelry, it behooves the buyer to know just what that word "gold" means to both the buyer and the seller.

Incidentally, another word about "pure gold" jewelry: in the nineteenth century there was a fad, enhanced by the discoveries of gold in California, the Yukon and Canada, for jewelry made out of gold nuggets. The natural nuggets were attached by rings to chains, soldered to stick pins or used as charms. (At the same time, and surely for the same reason, "fool's gold," or pyrite, a mineral which looks something like gold but has little or no intrinsic value, was also used widely in the same kind of jewelry.) Though people thought these were composed of 24-karat gold, the nuggets tended to contain quite a bit of matrix or other material; nevertheless, they are quite beautiful and often do have a high gold content. Thus, today these old nuggets, when they can be found, are quite valuable. However— and it is a big however—in the last few years nuggets have become voguish again, and unscrupulous opportunists (what other kind are there?) have jumped on the bandwagon with imitation nuggets cast in molds to resemble the real thing.

How can you tell the difference? Well, for one thing, fake nuggets, though they may indeed be made of gold, are *made*, and therefore have a uniformity, a smoothness of surface and material that is never found in a natural object. Sometimes, if they are carelessly finished, they may even have cast marks—little raised lines of gold that mark where the mold was seamed. If these have been polished off, there may be slightly brighter lines where they once were. Nothing in nature ever occurs quite the same way twice, and if you see a group of nuggets in which there are identical twins or triplets, you can be pretty sure they were made by man. And if the nuggets are hollow or show any signs of being worked on with a metal tool, you can be certain they are not the real thing. Finally, if you test them (more about this later) and find them to be either less than 18-karat or more than 22 (very unlikely) you have a right to be suspicious. The reason this is worth so much discussion is that a great deal of faked nugget jewelry was made within the last few years and is still on the market, being sold as 100 percent pure gold—and priced accordingly.

Testing gold is something that most people would not do themselves, but every good jeweler is equipped with a gold testing kit, acid and needles, and should be prepared at your request to test anything you buy which is certified to be gold.

Even if the gold is marked, it is perfectly acceptable to ask that it be tested in front of you (not in a back room where you can't see the results), and no good professional jeweler should take offense. Gold jewelry represents a considerable investment, and the buyer has a right to be assured that the article is as warranted.

When testing for gold, the jeweler usually uses a gold

testing kit, consisting of a stone, also called a touchstone, which may be of real stone or a special hard black composition; nitric acid; and a little fan of flat pointed triangles tipped with gold of various karats called needles or touch-needles. If the jeweler also has a file, beware. Often, to make sure that an article is gold all the way through (not rolled or plated), it is filed, and the exposed surface is touched with acid. If a greenish color is seen, the exposed metal is brass, and not gold. But the filed jewelry can never be completely restored. Filing, in my opinion, is like throwing the baby out with the bathwater.

The proper method for testing gold is to rub the article gently but firmly along the stone until it forms a *streak*. Then a similar streak is made using two needles, one of the same gold content as the piece is supposed to be, one of a higher or lower karat. The acid, which is kept in a tightly stoppered bottle, is then applied to the streaks. Streaks of the same karat fade equally fast. The jeweler may tell you that he doesn't have needles because they are too expensive (they are) but that he can tell by the speed with which a streak fades what karat gold it is. He may have that talent; some people do. But he may also be using weak or doctored acid. It is best therefore to have a control, either a marked needle or a ring or chain of your own, of known karat, to rub on the stone and compare. The higher the gold karat, the slower the streak is "eaten up" by the acid, and, in fact, 18K or higher gold usually leaves a mark that never entirely fades away. Low karat gold disappears almost as soon as the acid is touched to it.

Another way of testing for gold is to apply the acid directly to the gold. It will have no effect on pure or high karat gold, but will turn greenish if the gold is very low karat or brass. This is a much less sophisticated method and will not, despite what the tester may tell you, ascertain karat.

It would certainly seem that when gold is clearly marked

there should be no need to test it. However, particularly with jewelry whose maker is unknown, there have been exquisite frauds which fooled even the experts. I remember a beautiful basketweave gold bracelet, cunningly executed with the right color, weight and feel, and the legend 18K clearly stamped on the elegant clasp. This treasure had been given to my sister's daughter by an old boyfriend. She needed extra cash, asked my opinion of the bracelet, and wondered if I could offer it for sale to one of my friends in the business. I was glad to oblige, but when my friend saw it she looked abashed, and told me that she'd seen two or three like it in the jewelry district. Despite the real beauty and workmanship, it was not gold at all, but a clever fake. Imagine, the long-gone boyfriend probably never even knew he'd been sold a "lemon"!

Because of its malleability and tensile strength, gold can be easily worked in a variety of ways. It can also be heated and cooled many times over without shattering in a process called *tempering*, which restores the metal's springiness. It can be drawn into thin wire, woven into filigree or plaited into chains, bent into many shapes, melted to a liquid and cast or molded, covered with enamel, engraved with a steel tool either by hand or by machine (engine turning is a kind of machine engraving in which many straight, curved or zigzag lines are cut into the gold at one time), chased or textured with punches and hammers from the front, or repoussé—worked up into shape from the back. The ways in which gold can be used in jewelry are almost limitless!

The most desirable gold jewelry is of high karat, and handmade—that is, not molded or machine made but actually wrought individually and by hand. All handwork is very expensive, and even hand chasing or hand engraving adds to the price considerably. But it is worth it, because handwork adds not only to the beauty of the piece but to its value and charisma. One way to tell if a piece is hand-made is to ask. Another way is to look for telltale mold marks (there should be none) and to study the detailing through a magnifying lens or *loupe*. (Again, don't be embarrassed to ask your jeweler to let you use his or her loupe; every professional has one, and the really good jeweler should be glad that you care enough about the quality of what you are buying to study it so closely.) Machine-made jewelry has a uniform quality: each engraved line is exactly like the other. But handwork, no matter how skillful, is, when seen through a loupe, quite different.

In the case of high karat gold jewelry, which is elaborately engraved or chased, long and hard wear will eventually blur and finally erase the markings. However, there is something very wonderful about a fine gold piece that has that honorable mark of time upon it, and you should never, in my opinion, attempt to improve or recut old engraving to make it look new unless it has been absolutely erased. In this case, too, there is the strong possibility that it cannot be recut because the remaining gold is too thin. So what? Like white hairs and laugh lines, old gold should be treasured for what it is and what it has withstood, not demeaned by attempts to make it young again. All of this is to say that when gold wears it is not a sign of poor quality—in fact, quite the opposite. Many an old gold wedding ring has been literally grafted onto a new one as a thirtieth or perhaps even fiftieth wedding anniversary present. What a nice thing to look forward to when you buy a shiny new one!

Speaking of shine, gold jewelry can be washed in simple soap and water or, if very dirty, shampoo or ammonia, or even jewelry cleaner (though this is almost never necessary). It *should not* be rubbed with steel wool or abrasive cleaners, nor polished with regular metal polish that might have abrasive particles in it. Gold, as it ages, develops a lovely pattern of soft scratches called *patina* and in my opinion it should *never* be buffed up on a wheel or polished by a jeweler in such a way as to make it appear new. Often when you take a piece of jewelry in for repair a workman will try to do you a favor and polish it up. For me, this spoils it for the long time it takes to get it looking soft and worn and mine again. Another caveat: watch out for the careless or inexperienced craftsman who attempts to repair gold by soldering it with *lead solder*. Lead solder actually eats into the gold itself, eventually destroying it. Every gold piece must be soldered only with gold solder. The presence of a telltale grayish bit of lead solder is reason enough for a buyer to refuse or return a purchase.

Another hint about repairs: most rings need to be *sized* when they are bought, and most jewelers are equipped to do this work or have it done for you. However, most buyers are not aware that when a sizable chunk of gold has to come out of a ring, *it can and should be returned to you*. Gold is expensive; when you bought your ring you paid for the full amount of gold. Workers could make a fine living on just the gold they file away and cut away from pieces to be repaired—and some do. If you are having your ring sized, make sure—gently but firmly—that you get all the gold that's coming to you. And on the same subject: many fine gold watches come with their own gold buckles. Hardly anybody knows this—except the workers who replace watch straps. They often "cream off" the gold buckle without your ever noticing that it's gone, and simply replace the whole strap, including a cheap, nongold buckle. If you own a fine gold watch—particularly an older one—stop reading this minute and look at your buckle. If it's gold, make sure that each time it is replaced, you specify that you want your own buckle put on the new strap. If it's not gold...well, don't feel too bad. Maybe it never was.

Gold often turns fingers and, more embarrassingly, necks black. Actually it isn't the gold that is the culprit; it's the *alloy* that's combined with it—the same alloy that is eaten away by the testing acid to leave the real gold as a streak. To keep this black mark off skin and clothes, spray just the gold (avoid pearls or other soft stones) with any hairspray, thus giving it a light but effective coating. Obviously this won't work on rings, but hands are washed so frequently that the marks are usually not much of a problem there. Some people say they are allergic to gold and actually break out in a rash from contact with it. Since gold is inert, this seems unlikely, so perhaps the alloyed metal is the culprit again. Actually gold is so safe that it is used for earring wires—they should always be of gold, even if the rest of the earring isn't. I suspect that some of the "allergies" to gold rings are really irritations which develop under wide bands when hands are damp or soapy and not allowed to dry off. The cure for this is simply to take your ring off before washing dishes, and, perhaps, leave it off for a few days until the irritation heals.

Gold, gold, gold. How amazing a material it is. How much history it encompasses. How many people have fought and sacrificed and squabbled and literally died to possess it. And how ubiquitous it is; look around you—is there anyone who doesn't wear at least a bit of the beloved metal?

Silver

Gold is certainly the first-choice metal for most fine jewelry. But running a close second is soft, mellow, mysterious silver.

Like gold, silver is wonderful to work with—soft, malleable and strong. It can be beaten to an airy thinness, spun out almost miraculously into fine wire, and, though only about half as heavy as gold, has enough weight and substance to feel luxurious as tableware or adornments. But because it is so readily available—the commonest, in fact, of the precious metals—silver is much cheaper in price, and therefore not only easier to buy, but more appealing as a raw material to craftsmen who must invest their own money and time in their work before they make a profit. Silver's price, in fact, usually follows the rise and fall in the price of gold, even though its availability has nothing whatsoever to do with either the gold supply or with the myriad economic and political factors affecting the price of gold. Silver is always in good supply, and even, as happened recently, when it is monopolized and manipulated by profiteers, there's still plenty available. And it can be used for much more than just fine tableware and jewelry. Silver is important in industry and particularly in the manufacture of film—which, paradoxically, rose in price and never really came down after the great silver fiasco.

The irony is that what probably made the price of silver soar, besides the famous Hunt brothers, was the public's reaction to the escalating price of gold. Jewelry has become such a meaningful part of our lives that those of us who could no longer afford to buy gold turned to silver in numbers great enough to drive the prices up.

Though not as incorruptible as gold, silver is very resistant to tarnish; in fact, the problem of tarnish was practically unknown before the Industrial Revolution polluted the air. Suddenly the servants couldn't stop polishing. But since that same Industrial Revolution made it more difficult to get servants, silver declined in popularity. Many new cleaning agents and silver cloths are now on the market, but none will keep silver as tarnishproof as the manufacturers would have you believe. The only real way to keep silver from tarnishing is to plate it with another substance, such as rhodium; but this gives it a hard, glossy finish not unlike stainless steel, which, in my opinion, robs it of its beauty. My advice is never to buy rhodium-plated silverware or jewelry. For the slight convenience of not having to polish, rhodium plating robs you of the pleasure of watching silver age and develop its characteristic, beautiful patina. The soft pattern of light scratches (don't let this encourage you to do any heavy scratching!) which develops on silver after long use—and which cannot be duplicated by "brushing" with metal implements or scouring with harsh abrasives—actually adds to the beauty and value of silver, and to many people antique tableware and silver jewelry is even more desirable and valuable than brand new.

Silver itself is often used for plating, and the term *silver plated* is a common one. In the process silver is rolled out over a copper core in much the same way as rolled gold. Actually, silver plate is not much used in jewelry, since silver itself is relatively inexpensive. Usually, when you see silver-plated jewelry, it is *electroplated*, which means that a thin coating of silver is chemically deposited on base metal—a layer so thin that it wears off with the first hard use. Silver plating is not appropriate for jewelry, which should be able to be worn and cherished for many long years, and should never be bought—or sold—as a substitute for the real thing.

Unlike gold, silver is almost never found in natural nuggets, but as a component in ores that has to be smelted out. In fact, most of the world's silver is actually recovered as a by-product of the refining of other metals, like lead, copper, gold or zinc. Much is now mined in Mexico, where there is a particularly active silver jewelry industry as well. (The Mexican city of Tasco, or Taxco, calls itself "the silver capital of the world.") About a quarter of the world's silver comes from America, where it was originally used as an ornament by the Southwest Indians and is still worked and treasured (usually in combination with turquoise) by the Navahos. There are also large silver deposits in Central and South America, Canada and Australia.

Gold jewelry predates silver, and also lasts longer. Silver corrodes when it comes in contact with the earth, which is why so very little ancient silver jewelry still exists. But silver was definitely used and treasured by the ancients. A first century B.C. historian, Diodorus Siculus, even recounts his theory of how the inhabitants of Europe and Asia Minor in prehistoric times discovered silver when lightning or forest fires melted it out of the earth and left it in a workable lump. And we know that silver was being worked in Asia Minor as early as 4000 B.C., when all of the techniques for making silver jewelry, including chasing, engraving, piercing and soldering, were already in use!

In fourteenth-century England, the standard for sterling silver was set by the king, Edward I, to ensure the quality of the coins made of silver and the Church of England's ceremonial vessels. *Sterling silver* was defined as comprising 92.5 percent pure, or *fine* silver, with the remaining ingredients alloy, usually copper, added to harden the silver so that it would wear well. Edward decreed that all silver had to be *hallmarked,* or stamped with punches indicating its silver content, the city where it was made and the year. Sometimes, too, the manufacturer or silversmith stamped his own mark.

To this day, all British silver must be stamped in this manner, and the marks can be read even by the novice, with the aid of a small book of hallmarks (many bookstores carry them). What a thrill to study these small "pictures," letters and numbers through your looking glass and decipher the whole history of a piece of silver jewelry!

Though all countries do not demand as much of their silversmiths as the British, most do insist that silver be marked. So if you buy a piece of silver that is not stamped Sterling or has no numbers indicating the silver content (each country has its own notations) you should ask to have it tested. Like gold, silver can be tested right in front of you with chemicals to make sure that it is not base metal or, as is common in folk jewelry and ethnic jewelry, of very low grade.

In the United States, sterling silver must be 92.1 parts of silver to 7.9 of alloy. Much old Navaho jewelry was actually made from silver coins, which the Indians put on the railroad tracks so the trains could do some of their silversmithing work for them. This old *coin silver* is about 90 parts of fine silver to 10 of copper. The term *coin silver* occasionally appears on the backs of old silver pieces, and almost always is a sign of age.

Fine sterling silver jewelry that is worn frequently doesn't usually need to be polished. The friction of hands and skin is enough to keep it softly bright and assist it to a patina. But silver jewelry that is kept in a box or on a dressing table will eventually tarnish and need polishing. In the olden days, fine cigar ash was considered to be the best polish for silver, and it still is not a bad idea. It will not scratch or mar fine pieces, and will not stick in the cracks the way sticky liquid or cream silver polishes do. But in the absence of cigar ash, try ordinary kitchen cream of tartar, rubbing it on gently with a cloth or your fingers. A silver cloth made for polishing tableware is good too, or, if you are lucky enough to live in a city big enough to have a jewelry district, try asking for a *rouge cloth*, a flannel cloth impregnated with a fine polishing rouge that will not only keep your silver and gold jewelry in fine condition, but will wipe off and shine your watch crystal, the stones in your rings and pins, and pretty much anything else you apply it to. A rouge cloth will last just about forever, is inexpensive and will never scratch or mar your treasured possessions. If your local jeweler doesn't have one, perhaps he can send away for one for you.

There are many so-called silver dips on the market, but these are definitely not for polishing jewelry. They not only take off the tarnish that you *don't* want, but they also eat away at the mellowed dark insets of tarnish that give definition and beauty to your silver piece as it ages, and add to its patina. If you drop a piece of silver jewelry into one of these dips, it will emerge stark naked, stripped of all its individuality. For the small amount of work involved in hand-rubbing and hand-coddling your silver, you will gain a world of beauty, softness and value. In general, stay away from quick and easy methods unless your piece has been subjected to so much tarnish or staining that nothing else will restore it.

As with gold, if silver blackens your clothes or skin, try spraying it lightly with hairspray. Never paint your silver with colorless nail polish or a shellac-type lacquer. It will be ruined.

As a rule of thumb, the price of silver jewelry is about one tenth that of gold. But with the madness of our current inflation rates, it is hard to make any general statement about precious metals. It is not only silver's greater affordability, however, that makes it popular. For many women, particularly gray- or black-haired women or those with olive skin, silver is the most becoming metal to wear. In the summertime it gleams against a suntan, and the stones silver is usually combined with—turquoise, lapis lazuli, moonstones—may be your favorites. Very rarely is silver combined with precious stones (diamonds, emeralds, rubies, sapphires). The exception is antique jewelry, often used where silver was to set diamonds, instead of gold, since the whiteness of silver added to the diamonds' luster. The white metal of choice for precious stones is platinum (which I will speak of later) or less often, white gold.

As with gold, repair work on silver jewelry should never be done with lead solder, but with *silver solder*, which makes an invisible joining. Any silver jewelry which shows lead solder—darker in color, less shiny and softer than silver— has been poorly and cheaply put together.

Some people believe that gold and silver should never be combined, but I think that is nonsense. Gold is the symbol of the sun; silver, the moon. When put together tastefully, a twisted rope of gold and silver can be a rich and wonderful piece of jewelry. I know a woman of exquisite taste who always wears gold on her right hand, silver on her left. The effect is beautiful. If you like both silver and gold, don't feel you have to wear one *or* the other; you can creatively combine them, and the only rules are those of beauty, pleasure and personal taste. Two and three colors of gold have long been combined into exquisite jewelry; in fact, one of Cartier's best-selling pieces is a very simple three-color gold ring consisting of three interconnected rings that swivel around each other. If gold in its various forms can be combined, why shouldn't the same be true of silver?

And remember that silver is *not* a cheap substitute for

gold. It is in its own right a beautiful and versatile metal, with its own special qualities and personality, its own affinity for certain gemstones and certain people. If you are one of those people, count yourself lucky, and enjoy it!

More About Metals

In addition to gold and silver one other lesser known metal is commonly used in fine jewelry: *platinum.* While most people can easily recognize gold and silver, few can identify platinum. A white metal that bears a resemblance to silver and white gold, platinum is in fact "grayer" than either of them, without silver's soft patina. Platinum is an extremely hard and resistant metal, so there are very few scratches visible on its surface.

Platinum is actually one of a whole family of metals that includes *ruthenium, iridium, palladium* and *rhodium.* Platinum, the most often used on jewelry, has an extremely high melting point, but, once melted, is as ductile and easy to work as gold. In fact, some jewelers prefer it. It is most often used to set diamonds, and has been in fashion for diamond engagement and wedding rings since it was discovered in the nineteenth century—probably because its toughness ensures that the prongs of the diamond mountings will hold their precious cargo securely. In addition to holding diamonds, which benefit cosmetically from the reflection of its white metal, platinum is also used to set other precious stones, most often sapphires and emeralds. (The red of rubies, on the other hand, is set off more beautifully against yellow gold.) But there is something cold about the look of platinum, so it is almost never used without gems to make jewelry.

Traditionally, the price of platinum has stood just above the price of gold, like icing on a cake, and has fluctuated along with the price of gold. However, in the last year or two platinum has fallen below the price of gold. So now, in investment terms it is a "sleeper" and it is almost certain that, as the gold situation begins to stabilize, platinum and gold will again assume their traditional positions, with platinum on top. Nowadays the buyer should be able to specify "platinum, please" for a setting without paying extra. So, if you like the looks of this metal, enjoy!

The first source for platinum was in South American mines, and in the beginning it was extremely rare. In the twenties, though, copper and silver mines, first in Canada and then in South Africa began refining platinum, ultimately bringing the price down a little. In the twenties, too, yellow gold jewelry was not quite as popular, so platinum (and white gold) were used to fill the void.

Platinum is called a *noble metal*, which means that it is almost indestructible, and resists being eaten away by all acids except *aqua regia*, a mixture of nitric and hydrochloric acids. Thus, the best way to test a metal that looks like white gold and, when tested with nitric acid and gold needles responds like very high karat gold (the streak on the touchstone doesn't fade off), is to apply aqua regia to the mark. If nitric acid *doesn't* affect it, and aqua regia *does*, the piece is platinum.

To make the identification of platinum even more difficult, most countries do not demand that it be marked, including England, which does not have a hallmark standard for it. However, platinum, like gold, is usually alloyed with other metals (usually palladium, iridium or copper), with the proportion of platinum to the other metals at 95 parts to 100. Platinum is slightly heavier than gold (which is heavy enough!) and so a large piece of jewelry made of platinum—a wide bracelet or a massive necklace—would be very heavy indeed.

This should be a factor to consider if you are buying a costly necklace or bracelet, or even a large brooch, which will droop on your dress if it is too heavy. Often a clever goldsmith will set precious gems in platinum mountings (just as the old eighteenth-century goldsmiths used to set diamonds in silver) and make the rest of the piece in lighter, warmer-looking yellow gold.

The other members of the platinum family are also occasionally used in jewelry. Rhodium, you will remember, is often used to plate silver and protect it from tarnishing, but the result is not a very attractive one. Palladium is a fascinating metal that has never quite come into its own. Only half as heavy as platinum and about half the price, it is equally untarnishable and bright and has many good working qualities. Why it is so seldom used in jewelry is a mystery to me, but perhaps it will become more popular in the future. Whatever the reason, there is very little palladium jewelry in existence today. If you find a piece that looks and acts like platinum, tests like platinum, but is curiously light, perhaps you have stumbled on this elusive second cousin. Ruthenium and iridium, other members of the platinum clan, are used in alloying, and *osmium*, a lesser known platinum cousin, is never used in jewelry.

Though gold, silver and platinum are the primary metals used to make fine jewelry, there are a few other metals and materials that are used often enough to bear discussions.

Brass, also called *gilding metal*, is an alloy of copper and zinc, and is occasionally used for jewelry. Craftsmen work it by hand or mold it, taking advantage of its weight, its bright yellow color and its characteristic soft "antique" tarnish, creating liquid-looking pieces of considerable beauty.

Unfortunately, brass turns green when worn on the skin, and is thus unsuitable for chains and rings unless it is plated or coated. Brass earrings in particular should *never* be worn in pierced ears. In fact, *all* earwires should be made of noncorroding metals, such as gold or platinum, no matter what the rest of the earring may be composed of. Earwires of silver or brass, or even of gold plate (which may cover brass and wear off) can cause potentially serious irritations of the delicate ear area.

Brass is often used in primitive African or other ethnic jewelry. Usually it is easy to recognize this metal, but if you are unsure, drop a small amount of nitric acid on the piece in an inconspicuous spot, and if it turns green, you will know for certain that it is brass.

It is easy to polish brass with any one of a number of commercial polishes, but remember that since, like silver, its beauty depends partly on the soft patina it develops with age and use, dipping it in a polish that will eat up every bit of the patina is not a good idea. Brass can be protected from tarnish with light coatings of hairspray, or even with lacquer, if you don't mind the shine. It can also be waxed for protection, if the surface won't come in contact with anything that would rub off the wax. Though it is yellow, brass is no more like gold than ketchup is like blood. It is heavy like gold, but lacks gold's soft buttery luster and warm color. Overall, it is greenish, rather coarse in appearance (unless it has been highly polished) and tarnishes all too readily.

Bronze, an alloy of copper and tin (1 part tin to 8 parts copper) has been used since ancient times. Brooches of bronze were common even before 1000 B.C. In Anglo-Saxon times it was used for pins and buckles (mostly gilded), but today bronze is seldom used for jewelry except by a few craftsmen who enjoy working with its weight, solidity and characteristic "strong" appearance. In times like these, when the crafts movement is active, and new as well as old materials are being explored for use in jewelry, brass and bronze may once again come into their own.

Another metal you will sometimes come across in jewelry is *copper,* though most often it will be happily hidden beneath a colorful *enamel* coating.

Enamel was probably first developed to imitate the glow and color of gems. Imagine an ancient man or woman reaching into the cooled embers of a fire and picking out a glob of fused glassy brightness—an ornament easier to shape or drill or make than a gemstone, and often quite as beautiful. Glass, of course, has been used to imitate gemstones since before Egyptian times, and enamel is in fact powdered glass fused to another surface, usually metal. In jewelry the metals of choice are gold, silver and copper.

Since enamel is rather delicate and easily chipped, it is amazing that pieces of jewelry with enameling still visible have survived from the fifteenth century B.C. Gold ornaments of the Mycenaeans, rings from the twelfth century B.C. and a gold scepter from Cyprus were all decorated with this substance. The Greeks liked enamel set into *filigree* gold jewelry—gold wire woven into a kind of lacy pattern—and the Celts used enamel long before the Romans invaded Britain. Celtic enameling was always done in the primary colors—red, yellow and blue—and the metal used was usually bronze. In the sixth century A.D. in Byzantium, the art of enameling on gold or *electrum* (a mixture of gold and silver) became a complex technique involving intricate craftsmanship, and the influence of this eastern art penetrated into Europe during the so-called Dark Ages, influencing the jewelry and religious art of France, Germany, Italy and England. The enameling of the Middle Ages was superb and many pieces from this period can now be seen in the world's great art museums. Most people have heard of the famous Alfred Jewel, a ninth-century English enameled treasure; of Limoges enameling, a delicate variety of enamel painted on copper; of Bilston or Battersea boxes; or of Carl Fabergé, who delighted the prerevolutionary Russian court with dazzling enamel eggs, objets d'art and jewelry.

Today enameling is undergoing a renaissance, thanks to the popularity of small home kilns that enable the craftsman or hobbyist to create fine enamels at home. So this fragile art has survived the passage of time with style.

When you buy enameled jewelry today it is essential for you to know what kind of metal underlies the enamel. The very finest enameling is usually done on high karat gold, and is, of course, also the most expensive. The gold gives a warm sunny cast to the enamel colors, and sometimes a similar effect can be created by painting a copper background with a gold wash or covering it with gold leaf. The enamel colors on copper look more subdued, less brilliant, and enameling on silver creates a cold look that is most effective with colors like blue, green or black. Hand enameling is of course preferable to—and more costly than—machine work, and the more delicate the painting, the more coats of enamel and refirings needed for a certain effect, the more you will ultimately pay for the finished product.

Enamel is very delicate. Before you buy any piece of enameled jewelry, be sure to run your fingernail over it to make sure there are no cracks or chips. And remember that despite the fact that someone on your block may have a home kiln, enamel is very difficult to repair; if you buy an imperfect piece, it is likely to remain so forever. Very few jewelers will take on an enamel repair; so buy carefully, wear carefully, and you'll enjoy all your treasured enamel pieces for a long time.

Before we finish with the subject of enameling, let me add that there are five basic kinds of enamel you should be able to recognize:

Cloisonné, which comes from the same word root as

"cloister," or "cell," is a type of enameling involving the formation of cells or pockets of metal—usually gold—and the placement of powdered and colored glass inside to be fired and ground down and polished. The overall effect is of set gems, of colors in gold frames or pockets. Throughout time the Chinese have been the masters of cloisonné, often using it in brass for beautiful lamp bases, vases and jewelry as well.

Plique à jour is like cloisonné, except that, the back wall is missing; like a stained glass window it is, as the phrase indicates, "open to the day." This phrase, *à jour*, incidentally, is also used to describe a ring mounting that is open in back so that the stone lets the light of "day" shine through.

Champlevé is like cloisonné except that the cells have been *cut into* the underlying metal instead of being superimposed on it. It is much less common in modern jewelry than cloisonné.

Basse-taille, too, is enamel placed into recesses in metal, but in this method the recesses have first been chased or engraved with a pattern. Thus, basse-taille's variations of color and shading, can be quite beautiful.

Limoges, or *painted enamel*, is exactly what its name implies. Usually it is done by painting a white coat on a convex sheet of copper and firing it on, then drawing on the white background with a fine brush or palette knife in much the same way you would paint a picture in oils. The piece is usually fired in careful stages, so that the colors do not run together, and the exact depth of color and shading desired can be achieved. Portraits on enamel, painted boxes and the like are all painstakingly done in this fashion, and there are no limits to the rewards if there is enough time and talent to accomplish them.

In recent years jewelry designers, responding perhaps to the high price of gold and other precious metals, or perhaps to their own creative urges, have been experimenting with nonprecious metals for fine jewelry. I have seen extraordinary pieces in titanium, aluminum and stainless steel. But for the most part, if you are buying fine jewelry today it will probably be made from one of the good old standbys. Whatever the kind of metal, it must be strong enough to last and to hold its gems or enamel; the weight must be appropriate to the use (so you are not encumbered by a too-heavy necklace or pair of earrings), and it must not tarnish so badly that it loses its beauty. The price you pay must be appropriate to the beauty and art of the piece itself, as well as to the type of metal, which must be clearly identified to you before you buy it. And—most important of all—it must be a piece of jewelry that becomes you and pleases you.

The Precious Gems: Emeralds

What makes gems precious? The most obvious answer is the one we can all understand: price. And it seems obvious, too, that price is determined by rarity, beauty, size, clarity and so on. But buying a precious stone can be a very confusing venture. For many of us, the most important precious gem we ever choose is our engagement diamond—and what a trauma that choice can be! As expensive as a vacation, a car or even a house, this small bit of crystalline carbon can be a piece of art, a pledge of faith and an investment—but only if it is "really good," "really the best," "really worth the money." What do all these things mean? And how can you make sure your stone lives up to them? Don't despair. It needn't be as confusing as it may seem at first. And you don't have to be at the mercy of your jeweler either.

First, an essential definition: *diamonds, rubies, sapphires* and *emeralds* are the only stones defined as *precious gems.* Occasionally a new candidate is thrown into the ring—as when *kunzite* was discovered in California at the beginning of the century, or when a particularly fine specimen of topaz, spinel or aquamarine surfaces, and dealers wax poetic. But the truth is, these four gemstones—diamonds, rubies, sapphires and emeralds—are the only stones universally acknowledged as "precious." That is what we are going to talk about.

You might be surprised to learn that of the four, emeralds are usually the most expensive. A fine large clear emerald of good color and cut will bring more on the market than an equally large and equally fine diamond, sapphire or ruby. Why? Because emeralds are rarer than the others, more often have *inclusions* that mar the clarity of the stone, and are very rarely found in large sizes. There are many famous and huge gemstones that have been named and treasured through the ages, featured in royal crowns, fought over for collections, floodlighted in museums, but very few of them are emeralds. So if you own an emerald of the proper color and good cut that is reasonably clear of inclusions *(see glossary)*—even if it isn't large—you probably own a stone of considerable value.

The emerald has a long and mysterious history. As the birthstone for May, springtime's beginning, it symbolizes rebirth. The idea of birthstones, incidentally, started with the ancient Chaldeans, and the linking up of special gems with planetary influences. And the idea of protective stones and amulets can be traced to the beginnings of time. In Judeo-Christian tradition the Book of Exodus names the precious stones in Aaron's breastplate, and Revelations lists stones in the foundations of the New Jerusalem. In fact, many precious stones are named in the Bible, but in ancient times stones were identified by color and appearance alone, since there were no sophisticated instruments available to determine their chemical and physical properties. Also, some of the Bible's names for stones were lost in the translation, so it is often difficult to ascertain exactly what type of stone is meant.

The only thing we can really be sure of when an "emerald" is mentioned in the Bible is that the stone in question was green.

Nevertheless, emeralds were known to the ancients. The word "emerald" springs from an ancient Persian word, translated into Greek as *smaragdos*, and the earliest known emeralds were mined at the fabled Cleopatra's Mines in Egypt. These mines were active as early as 1650 B.C., and it is possible that all the emeralds of the ancient world may have had their origin there. In the Middle Ages, knowledge of the location of Cleopatra's Mines was lost, not to be recovered until 1818, when the mines were rediscovered. Since then, the emeralds taken from these mines have been inferior in quality—clouded and light in color—so, either the real location still eludes us, or the ancients' idea of a fabulous emerald was much less demanding than our own.

When Pizarro conquered Peru, along with the great stores of gold he also discovered the treasured Inca emeralds, which he promptly shipped back to Spain. Later the Spaniards discovered the source of the stones in the Andes, in what is now known as Colombia. Three great Colombian mines are still in operation at Muzo, Cosquez and El Chivor. The Muzo mine, with emeralds of a deep velvety color, is reputed to be the source of the finest emeralds in the world. Experts claim they can tell a Muzo stone just by its appearance. But there is another and, I think, more reliable way to identify these emeralds. Muzo emeralds have a characteristic inclusion: a flattish bubble of gas inside of which is a crystal, probably made of salt. Though this three-phase inclusion would be nearly impossible to see with the naked eye, a good ten-power loupe makes it visible, and lapidaries, using microscopes and other tools, can easily recognize and identify it.

Emeralds were discovered in Russia in 1830, when a peasant noticed green stones near the foot of a tree. The Russian emeralds were used a great deal in antique jewelry, but are seldom seen in this country today. They were often rather light in color, but some small stones had the prized deep green hue. Russian stones also have a characteristic inclusion: small bits of mica and actinolite.

India has been using emeralds for over a thousand years, but as far as we know, all the stones were imported. The first Indian emeralds were discovered in 1943, and in general are not of the highest quality. They can be distinguished by their inclusion of liquid-filled bubbles and the presence of biotite. Remember that these inclusions are minute, sometimes microscopic. It is the presence of many small inclusions, however, that makes an emerald look murky. Sometimes this murkiness, which is unique to each emerald's interior landscape, is quite beautiful, and there have been times in the past when emeralds with inclusions (like amber with leaves and bugs) were especially valued. This was true in the period of Art Nouveau jewelry (the end of the nineteenth century and beginning of the twentieth) when the cloudiness of a flawed emerald was thought to give the stone a mysterious and unique character.

Other countries, like Brazil, produce a few emeralds, and even the United States has emerald mines in North Carolina. But the bulk of fine stones on the market today come from Colombia. The government there is supposed to legislate the emerald traffic, but the truth is there is so little money in Colombia, and the stone is of such great value, that few controls seem to have any effect. Mining is arduous and dangerous. But, since emeralds are worth too much to blast out of the earth, they must carefully be recovered by hand. And any worker who slips an emerald crystal into his pocket and tries to sell it privately may not live to take the proceeds home.

Emeralds develop naturally in six-sided crystals. Therefore, as with all faceted stones, the cutter must take this crystal structure into account. He must also determine where the most pleasing color is in the crystal, and must try to get the best out of each piece. Color may vary, and, as we have seen, inclusions are almost always present, so you can see that the cutting of a fine emerald is a very delicate task. Emeralds are usually faceted in a *step* or *square* (really rectangular) cut called an *emerald cut*. In this cut, the *table*, or top *facet*, is flat, and around it are descending rectangular facets sloping down to the *girdle*, or widest part of the stone. Similar rectangles are cut below the girdle to the base facet, or *culet*. Then the corners are mitered. The emerald cut makes the most of a stone's color at the expense of brilliance, but since most emeralds do not have the lively flashing look of diamonds, this is usually not a great loss. I have seen magnificently "alive" emeralds cut in a round *brilliant cut* in the manner of diamonds, and there is nothing quite like them, but stones of this quality are few and far between.

Emeralds are members of the beryl family (hardness: 7½–8) the only precious stone in the group (which includes the lowlier morganite, heliodor and aquamarine). The finest color in emeralds is a deep green, not so dark as to be lifeless, but not so light as to appear yellowish or olive. The color is sometimes described as "grass green," but I think that is a misnomer, since grass is yellower than your best emerald should be. In fact, emeralds are *dichroic*—that is, two colors are present and can be seen when the emerald is viewed first from one side, then at right angles. One way the emerald is yellowish; the other, bluish green. The perfect color is a harmonic blend of the two, with the bluish green winning out by just a hair.

If the color is too light, the emerald lacks character and mystery. If it is too dark, the stone is murky and doesn't show up well at night, or under artificial light. If possible, before you buy an emerald try to view it in different lights: strong bright sunlight, indoor daylight, white north light and especially artificial light at night. You will be amazed at how alive your stone is, and how much it changes as the "sky" changes above it. Of course, most fine jewelry gets trotted out for special occasions, often at night, so it is especially important that you get a chance to view it under artificial light.

You may be surprised to know that many jewelers allow you to take a stone home with you for a few days and live with it before making a final decision. You might have to pay for the privilege by buying short-term insurance, or the jeweler may cover it for you. But the truth is that even a modest emerald represents a considerable investment of time, love and money. You owe it to yourself to make sure that this stone is the right one for you.

Most colored-stone merchants have one light they swear by, and a few sample stones they carry to compare to the stones they're considering buying. While you may not have these opportunities, it is wise to look at several stones at a time; in fact, you should *always* ask to see other stones when you are making a decision. You will be surprised at how the flaws and attributes of your choice will show up when it is in the company of its peers. As when you buy a puppy, you should choose the liveliest and brightest, the one most appealing to you—not necessarily the biggest, or even the "best buy." I am assuming, of course, that you are buying from a reputable and honest merchant who will guarantee *in writing* everything he tells you about the stone, including its *carat weight* and place of origin (if he knows it), and that it is a *genuine, natural* emerald and not a synthetic. The merchant should also allow, indeed *encourage* you to get an independent appraisal of the stone to assure you of its character and value.

It is hard to set a price on any precious stone since, as I have already mentioned, they vary with color, clarity and cut, size, supply and demand, and a variety of other factors that might influence their desirability at any given moment. A friend of mine who is a famous dealer in colored stones claims he can tell you anything about the politics and economy of a country by what stones its citizens are buying and selling—and for how much. Last year I paid a visit to him and found him at his desk surrounded by emeralds. "This is a terrific time to buy," he told me, handling a small fortune here, a large fortune there, as he fingered the gems. "The Iranians are dumping emeralds because they want to go home. The Colombians are dumping emeralds because they're trading them for drugs, condominiums and co-ops. If you want an emerald now, I could give you a really good buy!" At that time, a relatively large emerald, of about three carats, and of moderately good color, was on his desk for $11,000. Across the way, in Tiffany's, an emerald of comparable size and magnificent clarity and color, a really first-rate stone, was priced at $55,000. Today, with the Iranians and the Colombians no longer in the same straits, and inflation even higher, both stones would sell for far more. Incidentally, as with all other precious and semiprecious stones, a one-carat stone of fine quality might sell for one price; a two-carat stone of the same quality would sell for more than twice as much; a three-carat stone of equal quality for much more than three times as much; and so on. The bigger the stone, the rarer it is. This is especially true of emeralds. So if you want to invest in gemstones, get the finest quality, biggest, best-cut stone you can possibly buy. If your interest is not in investment but pleasure, choose color (and life) first, then size and price.

It seems to me that emeralds should really be the stones of engagement and marriage, since from earliest times they were reputed to change color to prove the constancy of a lover. Emeralds were also supposed to heal the blind, and to kill or blind snakes. They were said to possess charms against enchantment, so sorcerers could not weave their spells when in the presence of emeralds. And holding an emerald under your tongue was supposed to help you predict the future. Emeralds were said to strengthen the memory and sharpen the wits but they also were reputed to put out the fires of passion. There is an old legend about a king who, with his emerald on his finger, embraced his wife and cracked the stone into three parts!

Experts say that the first emerald stones to come from the mines are the biggest and most beautiful. The more deeply embedded they are in the earth, the paler the color and the more inclusions in the crystals. The stones are not found in riverbeds like diamonds, rubies and sapphires, but are fixed into the matrix rock, which means that the cost of mining these rare beauties is high. The matrix is often formed of pegmatite with layers of mica and schist, and it takes skilled, laborious work to free the precious emeralds from their bedrock. The emerald color comes from the presence of chromium; if you have ever thrown a glossy magazine into your fireplace to watch it burn, you will have seen the same magnificent blue green in the flames. Many of the emeralds you see today (both new and old stones) have been cut in India, where there is a centuries-old tradition of buying, cutting and selling the stones, and using the less beautiful material to be carved or tumbled into beads and cabochons. Some experts believe that the finest emeralds have already been taken from the earth, and as a result many modern emerald hunters have ended up with an antique stone to recut and refashion into a new piece of jewelry. Fine emeralds are becoming scarce, and in investment terms, this can only mean steadily rising prices. Unless a rich new source of supply is discovered and floods the market—a very unlikely event—the emerald you buy today, provided it is of fine quality and reasonable size, can only increase in value by tomorrow.

What happens if it is a *synthetic* emerald? All precious stones, emeralds included, have synthetic look-alikes, which sometimes can fool even the experts. There are some simple tests that you can do yourself to determine if a stone is synthetic, but these do not conclusively prove that a stone is real. Therefore, a good rule of thumb is: if your stone does not pass the test, reject it immediately; if it does pass, you should still take it to an expert lapidary (who will probably not give you an approximate dollar value), a qualified appraiser (who will), or best of all, The Gemological Institute or GIA, in New York City, where you will get a statement of authenticity (or nonauthenticity!), which is universally accepted.

The following are some of the tests you can do:

First of all, use your eyes—and your magnifying loupe. *Glass* is much softer than emerald (as mentioned, with a Mohs reading of 7½–8), so glass may be easily scratched or worn. If *any* scratches appear on the surface of your emerald, it may very well be just a cheap glass imitation. Emeralds, like all precious stones, are *cold* to the touch, so touch the tip of your tongue to the surface of the stone. Even a small emerald will be noticeably colder than a small bit of glass. And if the stone is large enough, drop a tiny bit of water on the surface. Water will bead up on all precious stones and flatten out on glass. I have seen some experts tap a stone on their teeth and claim they can tell glass from gem in this way.

As I said before, emeralds are dichroic, and in a stone of some size, a slight difference in the greens can be seen. Emeralds are also doubly refractive, which means that if an unmounted stone or a stone with an à jour setting is placed on a piece of white paper that has a pencil line on it, two lines will be seen through the stone. However, most emeralds are too dark to make this test a useful one for the average buyer. Like all natural stones, emeralds vary a certain amount in color, but glass or synthetics may vary too, so small color differences are not a sign of authenticity. However, almost all emeralds have some flaws or inclusions, so a perfectly clear, perfectly even stone is either a fake or a fabulous find!

A glass stone is not the only kind of fake you might encounter. Any precious stone that is not in an open mounting may be a *doublet* (a thin piece of emerald glued to another worthless substance like plastic or glass), a *triplet* (an emerald sandwiched between worthless slices of "bread") or a dyed or tinted emerald or other stone of poor color. If you study your stone through a loupe and see any signs of glue, suspect the worst. The stone may simply be glued into the mounting—a bad sign in itself—or it may be one of the cheats mentioned above.

A *synthetic* emerald, however, is not glass or plastic or dyed cheap material, but a real man-made stone, composed of the same chemicals as the real thing. However, the value of such a stone is far, far less than that of a genuine natural emerald, and you should never be sold a synthetic without being told exactly what it is. The Chatham emerald is quite a beautiful synthetic stone. Developed by Caryl Chatham and his son in San Francisco, California, around 1935, this stone, under a microscope or strong loupe, exhibits a feathery, veil-like pattern of inclusions, different from the tiny bubbles holding crystals of salt or pyrite characteristic of natural emeralds. Pierre Gilson, a Frenchman, also created a good synthetic emerald which also has an inclusion that is different from the one occurring in natural emeralds. Both the Chatham and Gilson emeralds exhibit a reddish color under ultraviolet light, while natural emeralds show no reaction at all. But more recent Gilson emeralds contain a small amount of iron, which prevents this fluorescent giveaway. Another kind of synthetic emerald, first produced in 1960, has a faceted piece of colored beryl as its "seed" or center, over which synthetic emerald is deposited, almost like the process used for a cultured pearl. These emeralds sold under the name of Symeralds can be recognized by immersing them in liquid; the two parts magically become visible.

Of course your very best protection in buying emeralds is a reliable, honest dealer. But no reputable merchant should object to your getting an outside appraisal, a report from the GIA if the stone is important enough to warrant it, and a complete sales slip guaranteeing that your stone is a genuine natural emerald, listing its size, carat weight and place of origin.

The Precious Gems: Rubies and Sapphires

Rubies and sapphires are grouped together like fraternal twins, because they are indeed from the same family. They are both forms of *corundum* (aluminum oxide), one of the hardest minerals, with a Mohs scale rating of about 9. Though the words "ruby" and "sapphire" bring to mind gemstones of blood red and brilliant blue, both of these stones have a wide range of colors. The ruby varies from shades of red to reddish pink, but sapphires have a broader spectrum of colors and hues. The depth and shade of the color is determined by the minute amounts of other minerals present when the gem is crystallized.

Of the two stones, the ruby has traditionally been more expensive, primarily because it is slightly more rare. But recently sapphires have been climbing in price and popularity. Of all the sapphire colors, blue is still the most popular, and the "correct" blue, the velvety cornflower color that is most preferred, is still the hardest to find and the highest in price. Perhaps the dazzling sapphire engagement ring that the Prince of Wales gave to his bride Diana last year captured lovers' imaginations. (After all, Charles's famous ancestor, Queen Victoria, made jewelry history with her engagement ring, too—an *oroborus*, or snake with its tail in its mouth, a symbol of eternal life.) The Japanese, the canny Arab gem buyers and the American collectors who sensed that sapphires were underpriced have all been snatching them up. As in the case of gold and silver, when the price of one of two related materials rises dramatically, the less expensive one gains in popularity until, in time, its price, too, is driven up. All the recent developments in the diamond world (which we'll discuss in the chapter on diamonds) have had this kind of domino effect on the prices of other precious gems, and since sapphires, though sufficiently costly, were at the bottom of this select heap, their desirability, and consequently their price, have soared.

Though I have heard various spirited arguments on this subject between dealers, the most prized sapphire of all is generally agreed to be the Kashmir sapphire, with its incredibly soft, deep cornflower color. These sapphires are exceedingly rare, as are their closest contenders, the Burma sapphires, which have a slightly edgier royal blue color. Ceylon, where most modern sapphires are mined today, is the home of a gem with a soft violet cast, as well as a great many *star sapphires*, which I'll tell you more about in a moment. Greenish blue and darkish blue stones are generally from Australia, and Thailand, the modern world's second richest source of sapphires, produces stones of beautiful clarity and bright blue color, which some experts consider to be the best.

And these are only the blue sapphires! Colors of sapphire can range from crystalline white stones which rival diamonds in their clarity (in fact, many diamonds were sold out of their mountings in the thirties and forties and replaced with clear "Depression diamonds," or white sapphires), to shades of yellow, brown, pink, violet, green and even black. However, though many of these stones are very beautiful, it is only the blue sapphire, and specifically the cornflower blue sapphire, that is really considered to be precious, thereby commanding a precious price.

Sapphires are strongly dichroic, which means that if you turn them you will see two colors, a violet blue and a greenish blue. In Ceylonese stones, the pink is often quite pronounced, resulting in a bluish violet stone that is, though less prized than a true blue sapphire, both provocative and, I think, very beautiful. Some sapphires have a "dead" look which to me negates even the finest color, while others truly have "life." A too-dark sapphire will look black under artificial light, so, as I've said before, when you make your decision, always make sure you get a chance to view your stone under a variety of conditions. As obvious as it may sound, it is easy to forget that a sapphire viewed under blue sky is really at its best; the same stone viewed at night may look dull and dark. Fluorescent lighting is kind to sapphires, as is the hard white light from a northern exposure. Most jewelers set up their gems on black velvet, which sets the gemstone off to its best advantage, and the artful lighting of showcases further contributes to the illusion of the stone's excellence, taking advantage of every facet and every glimmer. My gem dealer friend always wears a pure silk tie, and when he picks up a stone, he rubs it absentmindedly on the silk. Absentminded? Not at all! He's a gem lover, but he's also a gem dealer. The little bit of oil from his fingers might spoil a stone's glimmer, so he's doing everything he can to show his beauties off in their best possible "light." For the same reason, sapphires (except for antique pieces) are usually set in platinum or white gold.

As with all gemstones, the best way to view a sapphire is in a good bright light, preferably daylight, and in the company of other stones of comparable quality. It is also important—and don't be shy to ask—to look at your stone through a loupe. One view into the depths of a stone at 10X, or even 5X magnification, and you'll see why!

In all this discussion of gemstones, I have been assuming that the stones you want to buy are large, perhaps a carat or more. But many beautiful jewels are made with smaller stones, sometimes no more than chips. What is the criteria for judging these tiny stones?

First of all, make sure the stones are *not* chips—that is, that they are *fully faceted*. Small stones should be matched in color and clarity, of the same style cut, and matched in height, so that when you run your finger across the tops of the stones, they feel uniform in size and shape. Color is still very important, and the "massed" color of the stones should be as close as possible to the ideal—in sapphires, that velvety cornflower blue. Each stone should be carefully and individually set, and the prong of each small setting should be in place, so that each stone is securely held. These settings, too, when you run your finger—or even better, a bit of cloth—over them, should be smooth and uniform; any sharp edges may catch your clothing and eventually pull away, releasing the stone. Clearly the gems of the finest color will be cut into larger stones, if possible. But often gorgeous color comes in small packages, and by buying small stones you may be able to afford a color that wouldn't be available to you at a high price. Don't be afraid to seek out the very finest shade when you're buying small gemstones, and to insist on the same criteria of color, clarity and cut.

If it was recently mined, your sapphire probably comes from Ceylon, or perhaps Thailand, and its source was most likely in the gravel of an old riverbed. Rivers shift their course constantly, and like panning for gold, gemstones can either be sieved out of a river, or, more easily, dug from the debris on the banks. In Ceylon, a panner takes his supply of stones to a merchant who buys from all the miners, then passes the stones along to a cutter. At the cutting center, an expert in sapphires looks at all the crystals, trying to decide the best angle for cutting, where the best color lies or, if the stone is opaque, whether there is any good material inside. Sometimes a stone must be cut to determine if it is worth the attention given to a valuable gemstone; if it is not, it may be ground up and used in industry, or perhaps to polish other stones.

It is the cutter who makes the most critical decisions: how large the ultimate gemstone will be, which lines of cleavage to tap for the faceting, where the best color lies, how to cut to feature it, how to avoid the most prominent inclusions and whether the flaws in the stone will cause it to crack and splinter when the first taps of the mallet begin the delicate faceting process. Each question must be weighed against the others, even in the smallest faceted stones—and to a great extent the cost of a gemstone is determined by the time and expertise involved in the cutter's work.

Ceylon stones have a unique appearance, and since ancient times they have been cut with a deep bottom, or *pavilion*, with many facets. This means that Ceylon stones have a good deal of interior "life," but that they are heavier than other stones that may seem, at first glance, to be the same size. Since gemstones are weighed in carats, you will pay more for a Ceylon stone than for a shallower one with the same size *table*, or top, but the art of the Ceylon cutter is to bring a stone of any size to perfection. This might involve cutting many different sized facets, or planning how to keep the most intense blue color near the table or even before that, carefully studying the *rough* to determine how much is useless, how much can be cut into small stones (or *mélée*), and finally, locating the rare bit of wonderful blue that will eventually end up as a good-sized sapphire ring.

The sapphire is the birthstone for September and has been known since ancient times. Folklore tells us it was a symbol of wisdom. The Bible tells us that the Ten Commandments were carved on sapphire, but experts now believe that the blue stone referred to was probably lapis lazuli. However, the stone mentioned in ancient writings as "jacinth" or "hyacinth" probably was true sapphire. Because of its association with wisdom and purity, the sapphire, used in ecclesiastical rings, was believed to guarantee chastity; a sapphire that changed color was supposed to tell whether a woman had been faithful. Sapphire was also called "eyestone," believed to cure diseases of the eye, as well as to protect against poison.

The sapphires that come from Burma contain long needles of the mineral *rutile* that can often be seen with the naked eye and almost always with a 10X loupe. These woven strands look like—and hence are called—"silk." Kashmir sapphires, with their fabulous color, are often dulled by a foggy inclusion of tiny rutile fragments, and stones from Thailand tend to have small crystal inclusions. Burmese gems from the Mogok Valley have tiny fanlike inclusions, and American sapphires, from Yogo Gulch, Montana, have a distinctive type of liquid-and-crystal inclusion. I think that these small idiosyncrasies make gems more interesting. I always want to know all about the stones I buy—their history, their character, the place where they developed. In fact, I like to look at the gems through a microscope and "walk around" with my eyes through the unique pattern of inclusions that marks each stone as perfectly as a thumbprint. Sapphires tend to be clearer and have less "junk" inside than either rubies or emeralds, but it is rare indeed to find a stone of any size without any inclusions at all—and, within reason, these inclusions give character. It is only diamonds, of all the precious stones, that are expected to be absolutely flawless—and even they, under the high-powered jewelers' microscope—will often surprise their owners.

Having read the chapter on emeralds, you shouldn't be

fooled for a moment by a piece of blue glass that looks like sapphire. But there are a few other blue stones that might confuse you. *Tanzanite*, which was discovered in Tanzania in 1967, is a blue-violet stone that looks rather like sapphire, but is much softer (only 6 on the Mohs scale, in comparison to sapphire's 9). *Benitoite*, another recently discovered mineral, is a beautiful sapphire blue and has strong fire to it, similar to a diamond. It is a rare stone, occurring only in San Benito County, California, but if you do run across it, you can distinguish it from a sapphire by its comparative softness (only 6 on the Mohs scale) and, if you have a black light, by its tendency to fluoresce bright blue under shortwave light, whereas sapphire hardly responds to this kind of light at all. *Blue spinels* are sometimes passed off as sapphires, but they are usually much lighter in color and singly refractive—that is, if you looked at a pencil line through the stone in question, you would see only one line; with a doubly refractive sapphire you would see two.

At the end of the nineteenth century, the French chemical genius Verneuil introduced a way to make synthetic sapphires and rubies, a method that is used to this day: a furnace fueled by an extremely hot blowtorch fuses powdered aluminum oxide and coloring material (in the case of sapphire this is titanium and iron) into a glasslike *boule*, which is then cut and faceted into "gems." Synthetic stones tend to fluoresce strongly, and are therefore easy to detect. Also, if you examine them under strong magnification you can often see the curved structure lines; in natural stones the growth lines are straight, and follow the crystalline structure. Gas bubbles, rather like those in glass, are another tip-off to the prospective buyer that he's looking at a synthetic stone.

In general, synthetic stones may look very nice, but are not at all the same as natural ones, and any jeweler who tries to beguile you with nonsense like, "They have the same chemical structure as real stones; what's the difference?" should certainly not be trusted. The value of a synthetic stone is much less than that of a real one; but perhaps even more important, part of the mystique and wonder of a natural stone is its individuality, its beauty, and all the care and craft and passion—of man and nature—that brought it out of the earth, out of the hands of the craftsmen from foreign lands, to rest, blazing and safe on your finger. To claim that a synthetic stone is as precious as a real one is a little like saying a TV dinner is as good as a home-cooked meal.

Another way of faking gemstones—a method jewelers seldom discuss—is to apply heat to stones of poor color to develop a look that is more marketable. Most sapphires, when they are mined, are an unappetizing milky gray; the blue stone, or even the clear-colored stone of any hue, is a rarity. These ugly stones, called *geudas*, are sometimes subjected to experiments in which heat is applied to improve color and clarity. The dealers in Hong Kong and Thailand "cook" geudas to make them more marketable, heating them up to about 1,700° centigrade. This technique either ruins them or results in stones of a better hue, usually yellow or blue. Now these heat-treated sapphires *are* genuine natural sapphires; all the tests will prove that. So how are you to know if they have been treated? And does it really matter?

Well, it matters to me, because part of my pleasure in a gemstone is the astonishing set of natural coincidences that contributed to its creation. But I can see the other side of the argument. The digging and cutting and polishing and selling of any stone are certainly not "natural" or coincidental. No gemstone ever leaped, fully faceted, into its owner's palm! But nevertheless, a treated stone is generally considered in the business to be faked and the price should reflect that fact.

Cooked stones do not lose their color over the years as dyed ones sometimes do. And heat treating of aquamarines has become so common that when you see a particularly good one you should assume it has been cooked. Star rubies and sapphires, which I will discuss in a moment, often have had some treatment to improve their appearance, and sometimes heat treating can even change or improve inclusions. The issue of cooking a stone can perhaps be compared to getting a face-lift. Is it wrong to deceive, or is it a legitimate cosmetic procedure, solely designed to enhance beauty and pleasure? Well, I would rather have a totally natural stone, and I always ask the question directly: "Has this stone been heat treated or dyed?" and make sure that a GIA certificate accompanies each major gemstone purchase. But the sad truth is that many dealers don't know, or don't always want to know, the history of a stone—and many don't consider it necessary to tell you even if they do.

Irradiation of sapphires is another matter, because the blueness that it causes is temporary, an illusion that will fade over time. Another way of faking sapphires is to immerse them in a special chemical powder and heat them. Only the surface improves in color, and though this improvement is permanent, if the ruse is discovered by the GIA or another gemological lab, or if the stone is ever recut and the less desirable color appears, there will be some embarrassed faces...and a big drop in the stone's value.

I hope all this talk of faking and altering won't discourage you from buying sapphires or any other precious gem. As in choosing a partner in marriage, there is a certain amount of *caveat emptor* (let the buyer beware) necessary. But, also like marriage, the pleasure that can be expected is well worth a little extra care and thought in the choosing. Every major jewelry purchase should definitely be appraised, and every major gem should have a GIA or equivalent certificate as well. Make this clear to your dealer from the beginning, and he will not only respect you more, but will be less likely to fudge or "forget" or conceal any important facts about some stones.

Asterism is the starlike effect resulting from the way light hits the small fibers and inclusions within some stones. Rubies and sapphires produce the finest "stars," and beautiful *star rubies* and *star sapphires* are prize possessions. They are always cut *en cabochon*, meaning with a rounded top and a flat bottom, to emphasize the star, and are usually mounted in rings. Most often the stars have six or twelve rays, of more or less "whiteness" or clarity. There are other stones which sometimes display asterism—rose quartz, garnet and spinel among them—but they are rare. Like other rubies and sapphires, star stones may have been synthesized, played with and enhanced by dyeing or cooking. Since they are so rare, and command a high price if the star is strong and the color of the stone is good, it is important to ask the same sharp questions about them.

Much of what I have said about sapphires applies to rubies as well, and perhaps I have spent more time on the "true-blue" stone because I actually like it better. But goodness knows, rubies have their staunch admirers, too, so let me tell you a few things about what the ancients called the "king of gems."

Rubies have the same basic composition as sapphires, with one difference: their coloring material is chromic oxide. This produces a red ranging from palest pink to the most prized pigeon blood color, passing through tints of purply violet and orangy red. A flawless ruby of good size and color is even rarer than a comparable sapphire, and will cost more. In fact, allowing for the unpredictable nature of the gem market and the vagaries of styles and taste, a fine ruby of good size will generally cost more than a diamond of equal size and quality. Star rubies are even rarer than star sapphires, and more highly prized, especially if the stone is of a good color and the star is well-centered and bright.

The process of mining rubies has not changed much since prehistoric times, and in fact, ancient tools for cutting out the crystals have been found in what is still considered to be the site for the finest rubies, the Mogok tract in upper Burma. In the eighteenth century this site was thought to be so dangerous that it was used as a place of exile, and the prisoners were sent to work there as a punishment. The precious rubies are still dug by hand in the most primitive way, native miners being lowered by pulleys down "wells" or narrow shafts to a depth of ten to thirty feet. Often a family works together, scraping up layers of the gem-bearing gravel, called *byon*, and hauling it to the surface. When the day's work is done, the miners pick their gravel over for gems. It is a tedious, risky business, made more dangerous because there is almost no legal protection for the workers, no central market for buying and shipping the gems, and no cutters on hand at the mining site to determine the real value of a gem. The miners, who repeatedly risk their lives to recover the precious bits of crystal, are often robbed, cheated and even killed for their trouble. But they are virtually powerless, since the centers for cutting and marketing the gems are so far away, and so they sell to whomever is at hand, at whatever price is offered.

Considering all this, isn't it amazing that any gems at all manage to make it to your local jewelry dealer? In fact, so few really fine large rubies are mined any more that the experts usually are aware of any special find and can trace its course—by rumor if not fact—as it travels from mine site to cutter to market to designer or setter, and finally is put up for sale. Like all precious gems, the shortage of prime material may mean that a new gem is really an old one, taken out of its setting and reused, or perhaps recut and repolished to "new" brilliance. Like the gold in your ring, your gemstone, too, may have a long, long history. Thus, it is worth asking about if your stone is a large one.

While its history, or *provenance,* would probably not be known by an appraiser or the GIA, the person who bought it and then sold it to you might be pleased to share its story.

It goes without saying that in all colored stones as well as in the diamond, clarity is a must for top value. If a diamond is an "off" color, most often a trifle yellowish, its value is diminished. But the real concern for diamond dealers, the factor they argue about, study, spend sleepless nights worrying about, is the stone's degree of flawlessness.

In the case of colored stones, though clarity is important and adds to the lively look of a stone, *color* is crucial, and since no photograph, adjectives or measurements can really express the subtle shadings and variations and tinges and tones that are possible in each unique product of nature, colored-stones dealers spend hours arguing, worrying, studying and trying desperately to remember all the stones that have passed through their hands to compare and classify and value "perfect" color. For a ruby, that color is called "pigeon blood." But what does that mean? The redness, caused by the presence of chromium, varies to an infinite degree with each variation of a gem's chemistry. Moreover, as we already know, the light under which a stone is viewed changes its color; and remember, clear, smogless sunlight in Ceylon or India is not the same as the cloudy, polluted sunlight of London, Paris or New York. Ruby color is not as sensitive to the light as is sapphire color, but it certainly is crucial to view a stone in the best light possible, and in the presence of as many stones of similar quality as can be assembled. And even then, dealers will argue endlessly about the origin and quality of ruby color. However, there is a general rule-of-thumb that will enable you to use color to judge a ruby's origin.

A *Burmese* ruby at its best is a full rich red with a slight touch of orange, rather than blue. This is the true "pigeon blood" or "Burmese red." If the stone is blackish or bluish it is less valuable. A *Siamese* ruby usually has slightly more purple, and is often very brilliant and "alive." A *Ceylon* ruby is usually pinkish, and an *African* stone often has a brownish cast. But these small differences are hard to distinguish unless you are an expert. The inclusions in a ruby are a more reliable indication of its birthplace. Although experts may argue about whether a color marks a stone as Burmese or Ceylonese, tiny crystals of rutile (called, as in sapphires, "silk") instantly identify a Ceylon gem. African and Thai rubies very often show a pattern of tiny parallel "stress lines," and rubies from India, Australia or the United States show characteristic inclusions as well. A trained lapidary or appraiser can read these unique thumbprints for you and tell you where your gem was born.

Synthetic rubies were first marketed in 1908, and threw the ruby market into a panic. However, they have never really affected the price or desirability of true natural rubies, primarily because they are so easy to detect. They fluoresce an electric pink red under black light, and their daylight color borrows from this shade. Once you have contrasted the bright, glassy luster of synthetics with the richer, mellower look of real ruby color, the fake and the real will be clear to you.

Spinel, a natural stone that looks very much like ruby, is a different matter. Throughout history, fine red spinels have been mistaken for rubies, and even in the sanctity of museums and throne rooms, "rubies" have been unmasked to be spinels. The spinel has a peculiar shade, either a raspberry or an orangy red that should be a dead giveaway, but often isn't. The famous Black Prince's Ruby is in reality a spinel (also called a "balas ruby"), as are many of the "rubies" in the national treasure house of Iran. The most measurable difference between spinels and rubies is in their hardness: spinel's 8 contrasts with ruby's 9.

Another stone that is commonly confused with ruby is the *garnet*, a semiprecious gem that comes in a blood red color, but is neither as lively nor as hard as the ruby. Garnets are also not dichroic, as rubies are, and have no fluorescence under a black light. Natural rubies do fluoresce (though not as spectacularly as synthetics).

Rubies are the birthstone for July, and are associated with blood and fire. In ancient times people believed that a fire actually shone in the heart of a ruby, and thought that if it was a true ruby, when placed in water it could make the water boil! It was treasured as a talisman of peace and a protector of life and property, but only when worn on the left side of the body.

With today's inflation and the subsequent insecurity of dollar investments, more and more people are looking to gemstones and jewelry as a hedge against rapidly rising prices. It is a fact that the price of gold and the price of bread have maintained a congruent relationship for centuries. When inflation drives the value of a dollar down, rubies, emeralds, sapphires—*real* goods as distinct from paper money—float upward and even gain in value, as people try to buy them and squirrel them away against an uncertain future. In our discussion of diamonds, we will see that the price of these beauties has long been controlled by an international syndicate. However, rubies, emeralds and sapphires—the precious colored stones—develop in too many different places and are controlled by too many different interests to be easily manipulated in this way. So the colored stones, with all their variations and endless fascination, also seem to me to be the best bets for investment buying. Of course any investment must be made cautiously, and with the help of experts. And you are more likely to get the most for your money by buying the very best you can: the very best color, the most life and clarity, and the greatest carat size you can afford. My colored-stones expert always warns me against buying a piece of jewelry with many small stones for investment, since, except for antique jewelry, the major resale value of a piece lies in the quality of the major gem. The remaining parts of the piece—the gold or platinum mounting and small accompanying stones—account for only a very small part of the dollars spent. Only in the case of jewelry that has been made by a famous craftsman (and there are very few today whose names really count for dollars on resale), or in antique jewelry, where excellence of design and workmanship as well as age and condition also affect price, is the major gem *not* the determining factor in the piece's resale value.

If you do decide to invest in colored stones and/or jewelry, you must also be prepared to hold on to your treasures for a while, since when you buy you pay retail price, and when you sell, you often sell at wholesale. But even with these sometimes risky conditions, gem investment is an fascinating and enriching aspect of many people's lives. There is always a market for fine gems. If you take good care of them, they will never wear out. They don't need maintenance, aside from an occasional cleaning (or, in the case of jewelry, a possible repair) and they never really go out of style, because jewelry styles change very slowly, if at all, and "period" jewelry is, if anything, even more desirable and popular than today's designs.

In short, owning and enjoying and wearing precious gems is profitable for your heart as well as your purse, designed to bring you pleasure, joy, a lucrative investment...and, who knows, maybe even a little magic!

The Precious Gems: Diamonds

Volumes have been written about this fiery, fascinating and most volatile of the precious gems. And yet the whole story has never been told. For unlike emeralds, sapphires and rubies, diamonds—though beautiful, expensive and durable—are not really rare. More than any other gem or precious metal, they have been manipulated into a position of desirability and scarcity by the De Beers Corporation, a huge international cartel that owns and controls nearly all the diamonds in the world. But even as these words are being written, the power of that immense diamond monopoly may be crumbling, and the future of the diamond is dizzingly uncertain. "Diamonds are forever" is the advertising message De Beers has been broadcasting to the world since 1948. If that means that they *last* forever—that their adamantine hardness (at the top of the Mohs scale, 10) and imperviousness to acids, heat or corrosion make them practically immortal—then, with a slight bow to permissible puffery, the statement may be true. But if, as most of us have been led to believe, it means their *value* lasts forever, then we all may be in for a bit of a shock. But before we get to price, let's talk a little bit about the other, and very real qualities of diamonds that have made them desirable long before De Beers's empire came into being.

Diamonds are the hardest natural substance in the world. Curiously enough, their chemical composition, carbon, is shared by one of the softest: graphite. The difference between a clear, sparkling diamond and the dull gray, greasy substance used for greasing locks or as the "lead" in pencils, is the tremendous heat and pressure deep within the earth. The crust of our planet, the part we live on, is only a small, relatively thin surface. Below this crust is a boiling cauldron of magma which occasionally bursts through a weak seam in a volcano of molten rock or lava. Sometimes when these pipes of liquid magma cool and solidify, they form *kimberlite*, a blue green or grayish ore in which carbon, miraculously transformed by the intense heat processes it has undergone, crystallizes into diamond.

Who is to say that the ugly duckling has been transformed into a swan? Is it just the De Beers empire that tells us these fiery crystals are beautiful and desirable? Hardly. Diamonds have intrigued man since earliest times. Legend has it that in ancient India diamonds were worn as talismans or magic stones. In the first century A.D. Pliny the Elder declared that only kings and emperors could wear them because they were so hard, so rare and so valuable. They also had magic, he said: swallowing a diamond would counter the effects of poison, and when worn, they would protect the wearer against insanity and the perils of war. The best way to prove a stone was a diamond, said Pliny, was to hit it with a hammer. How wrong he was! Hard though they are, diamonds will chip or splinter with a blow.

Throughout the ages, diamonds have been prized by great leaders. Charlemagne, who loved jewels and forbade the old custom of burying them with their dead owners, owned and wore many diamonds. When Marco Polo visited the court of the great Kublai Khan in the thirteenth century, he returned with fabulous stories of the mountains of diamonds he had seen in the Orient. Shah Jehan, the Indian mogul who built the Taj Mahal, loved diamonds so much that he had first rights to any stones from the famed Golconda mines. And, in fairness to the diamond, we must remember that these early stones were uncut, or nearly so. The diamond is so hard that no other substance will cut or polish it, and the secret of how to do this was not discovered until later. Unlike any other gem, the beauty of the modern diamond is determined by its *fire*—the dispersion of light, that fracturing of white gleam into rainbows of twinkling color that is brought about by artful, careful faceting. Other stones have color; the diamond's uniqueness lies in its clarity, its lack of color. In its natural state the diamond is most often a grayish, unimpressive bit of crystal, perhaps an octahedron, perhaps a waterworn pebble or a fragment. So, even in earliest times, these clear, hard carbon fragments must have been compelling enough to inspire such awe, love, respect and passion!

In the fifteenth century Louis de Berquem, a brilliant Jewish artisan from Bruges, Belgium, took what was then known about polishing diamonds—mostly that rubbing them with a combination of olive oil and diamond dust produced facets and luster—and, after moving to Paris to study mathematics and proportion, used what he had learned to become the finest diamond cutter of his day. His statue still stands in the heart of Antwerp, which he helped make into one of the world's great diamond centers. By the time of Cardinal Mazarin, the prime minister to Louis XIV of France, known for his love of diamonds, the great stones were traditionally polished and faceted into the *single cut*, sometimes called the *Mazarin cut*: an octagonal flat top (table) with eight facets above the rounded "waist," or "girdle," and eight below.

A seventeenth-century Venetian, Vincent Peruzzi, developed a new way of faceting which involved an octagonal table, thirty-two carefully planned facets above the girdle, twenty-four below it, and a *culet*, or flattened end, at the base. Evolved from this model is today's most popular faceting called the *brilliant cut*. Peruzzi's genius becomes clear when we realize that before this model was devised, none of these early "cuts" were actually *cut* at all. With all the devilishly ingenious engineering that these early craftsmen brought to diamond faceting, they never figured out how to actually *saw* a stone, so all their "cutting" was actually *grinding*: working away tediously and patiently at the incredibly tough diamond with olive oil and diamond dust, wasting huge amounts of the original material in their attempts to wear it down by the use of their hands and a primitive grinding wheel to the most pleasing shape and form. It wasn't until the eighteenth century—the Age of Diamonds—that a method for sawing the adamantine stones was devised. In this vein I should also mention *cleaving*. An early method still used today to facet diamonds, cleaving is a heart-stopping operation in which, after carefully studying a diamond's internal structure, a master cutter marks the point at which he believes the diamond, if properly struck, will fracture cleanly. A thin ridge is then grooved into the surface of the stone and a cleaving knife is carefully placed in the ridge and tapped with a palm-wood hammer or a special rod. If all the calculations are correct, the diamond will cleave perfectly; if not, it may shatter into bits.

As you can imagine, there is plenty of folklore about the miracles and disasters engendered by this perilous, amazing act. One popular story tells of the great Lazare Kaplan, who was chosen to cut the Jonker diamond. This stone was picked up in 1934 in Pretoria, South Africa, by a hitherto luckless miner, Jacobus Jonker, and that night his wife slept with it to keep it safe from discovery. Later, the huge stone, about the size of an egg, was sold to the Diamond Corporation (a branch of De Beers) for $315,000, mailed to London (postage: 64¢!) and shown to Harry Winston, a famous—and flamboyant—jewelry merchant in New York, who bought it for a rumored $700,000. It weighed 726 carats—the seventh largest diamond ever found—and was exhibited at New York's Museum of Natural History and in six other cities of the world before Winston brought the stone back to America. In the meantime, he had consulted Europe's master cutters as to the best method to divide this fantastic diamond, to get the finest, clearest, most fabulous stones. Then Winston consulted Kaplan, a former Belgian living in New York who, like his famous former countryman, Louis de Berquem, had a well-deserved reputation as one of the world's finest cutters. Kaplan offered an ingenious new solution which, if it worked, would result in eleven emerald-cut stones, one of which would be very large, as well as one marquise-cut gem. To carry out this plan, Winston chose Kaplan. After months of study, Kaplan marked the stone with India ink, took a weekend off to go trout fishing, and then came back, set the blade in place and struck hard. The diamond fell into exactly the pattern he had predicted. Bystanders say that the cleave was so perfect that there actually was ink left on both sides of the cut. Gossips claim that afterward Kaplan fainted. It doesn't take much imagination to conjure up how Kaplan must have felt, knowing that as the hammer went down millions of dollars worth of irreplaceable gemstone hung between disaster and triumph. As a matter of fact, the largest of the Jonker gems, an emerald cut of 125.65 carats called the Jonker diamond (the largest emerald cut in the world to date), was later sold by Harry Winston to King Farouk of Egypt, repossessed and resold to the queen of Nepal and, after dropping out of sight for years, this stone resurfaced in Hong Kong and was sold to an unidentified Japanese businessman for a reputed $3,500,000.

Though newer, more sophisticated measuring implements have been devised since that time, new cuts invented, and some improvements made in calculating the precise angles and sizes of facets, the basic design offered by Peruzzi three centuries ago is still used today, and the round brilliant-cut diamond is still the most popular for jewelry and for investment.

Other variations of the brilliant cut are the *pear shape* (or *pendeloque*), the *oval*, the *marquise* (pointed oval, or *boat shape*) and the *heart shape*. These are all planned with triangular or trapezoidal facets. In the *step cut*, or *emerald cut*, with its variants (*square cut*, *baguette cut*) the facets are arranged in rectangular steps or rows above and below the girdle. This cut creates the illusion of the greatest size, and loses the least amount of weight in the cutting, but is really only suitable for large and extremely clear stones (except, of course, for the baguette, which is traditionally used for small side stones). The emerald cut, besides being unusual looking, seems to say "size" and "perfection" to most people, so sometimes an inferior stone that is emerald cut will fool you into thinking it is of higher quality than it actually is. Perhaps this accounts for the emerald cut's popularity.

The first diamonds were found in India, in riverbeds or loose alluvial soil, and it wasn't until much later that diamond mines were discovered and the finding of diamonds become more than just a happy accident. By the time of Alexander the Great (fourth century B.C.) there were already tales of diamond mines in India, fiercely guarded by snakes and demons. The earliest diamonds we know of in jewelry were used by the Romans, but they were uncut and looked nothing like their flashing counterparts of today. Our early ancestors believed that diamonds cured poisoning and protected their owners from the plagues and pestilences that ravaged Europe. If worn against the skin, they were said to be a charm against nightmares and to ensure peaceful sleep. Diamonds were thought to be a symbol of purity and truth, and a guard against the evil eye—but only when given as a gift. It is possible that this explains why diamonds are traditionally given as engagement rings today. But I tend to think that this custom, too, we owe to the public relations acumen of the De Beers conglomerate, since it is a practice that became popular toward the end of the nineteenth century, just as De Beers's fortunes were on the rise.

In the Middle Ages, natural pointed diamond crystals were mounted in rings and used throughout the Renaissance by lovers to scratch their initials or names on panes of glass. In those days scratching the stone against glass was considered a test to determine a true diamond. Most diamonds were mounted in silver, even if the rest of the piece was gold, to give them a better color, and they were often "foiled," that is, backed with a thin bit of silvery, or sometimes even painted, metal. The settings were closed, and the cut—if it wasn't simply a polished, pointed crystal—was either flat, or *table cut*, in which the top facet was simply ground down flat. Another popular early cut, which dates back to the sixteenth century and was popular even in the nineteenth, was the *rose cut*, in which the top of the stone is domed and covered with triangular facets, while the bottom is flat. But these early diamonds, while they are attractive, bear little resemblance to the dazzling, sparkling diamonds of today. Peruzzi's ingenious brilliant cut accentuates the two most extraordinary qualities of the stone: *color dispersion*, and *high refractive index*. Light entering a well-cut diamond is broken up into all the colors of the rainbow, producing the "fire" we all associate with this gem. Even a tiny stone, if it is full cut, sparkles and winks with a multicolored light that is dispersed throughout the stone. The high refractive index means that a large amount of the light hitting the gem is held and reflected within it, so that the stone itself seems to flash with light. The combination of fire within and fiery glimmers thrown outside, plus the diamond's fabled hardness, its high price and mystique, all give the stone its glamorous personality.

The favorite diamond color is an absolutely clear water-white, but other colors are known, including pink, blue, brown, yellow, red and green. These are called *fancy* diamonds and, though their value is somewhat unpredictable, in recent years it has been of comparable and occasionally even greater value than clear stones. The fabled Hope diamond is an incredible blue, the largest blue fancy in existence, and its fame dates back to the seventeenth century. That 44.50 carat beauty now resides at the Smithsonian in Washington.

So-called "colorless" diamonds do have faint tinges of color, but these are usually evident only to the trained eye. A faintly bluish color is preferred to a yellowish color—but if the blue is caused by blue fluorescence, fairly common in diamonds, it is less admired than if the stone itself has a slightly bluish tinge. The term "blue white," however, is really misleading. The stone you want to buy is "pure," white, "clean" or "of the first water."

The most important diamond mines in early times were the famed Golconda mines near the river Kistna in India. These are all but worked out now. The discovery of diamonds by the Portuguese in Brazil in the 1700s caused quite a furor. Diamond merchants feared that this rich new source would harm the stone's reputation for rarity, and quickly spread the word that the new stones were inferior. For some years the Brazilian stones were shipped to India and sold as Indian diamonds. By the time the ruse was discovered, Brazilian stones had become established, and these same mines, in Minas Gerais, as well as new deposits at Bahia, are still being worked by primitive methods today.

It was in 1866, on the banks of the Orange River in

South Africa, that the whole course of diamond history was changed. A farmer's children brought home a pretty pebble. That was finally identified as a 21-carat diamond, the Eureka. Three years later an even larger stone, the 83-carat Star of South Africa was found in the same area, and the diamond rush was on. The earliest miners found the gems in loose surface soil, but later the great volcanic deposits of kimberlite of the Kimberley, Wesselton and Premier mines and others made diamond mining in South Africa big business. In a historic struggle for power, Cecil Rhodes and Barney Barnato, two English adventurers who had both struck it rich in the diamond fields, finally achieved an uneasy merger which resulted in a virtual diamond monopoly: De Beers Consolidated Mines. Together with its London connections, De Beers successfully controlled the flow of diamonds to every country in the world, and the price that they would bring in every market.

As diamonds were discovered in other parts of Africa and in other countries, De Beers extended its influence until the corporation was responsible for the mining, sorting and marketing of 85 percent of the world's diamonds. In countries where their corporations—doing business as the Diamond Trading Company, the Diamond Corporation, the Diamond Producers' Association, Industrial Distributors (Sales) Ltd., the Central Selling Organization and possibly under many other names—do not actually own the mines, they buy up all the diamonds that are taken out of the ground, hold them, parcel them out as they determine and keep the supply of stones low and the price high.

In fact, gem diamonds are not truly rare in the same way that rubies, sapphires and emeralds are. They are, believe it or not, about as common as garnets. But the De Beers policy, coupled with the De Beers advertising, which informs us over and over that "Diamonds are forever," and that this stone and this stone alone is the rarest, the finest, the most suitable for a gift of love, has been sold to people all over the world, making De Beers an incredibly rich and powerful cartel, with the merchants and brokers who are part of its elite chain becoming controllers of the entire diamond industry.

Until now. Within the last year shifts in the economy coupled with new, rich diamond finds have shaken De Beers to its foundations. The De Beers system only works if there is a rigid control of both supply and demand. By keeping a tight hold on the world's diamond production and distribution, all the while fueling the consumer desire for this gem, De Beers could steer diamond prices as effectively as if there were only a few dozen gemstones found in the world each year. But when the Soviet Union and then Australia discovered huge new diamond deposits, supply and demand began to swing out of the corporation's control. In addition, during the last few years as diamonds were touted as a safe investment, and as inflation drove the dollar down, more and more people began putting their money into seemingly "safe" stones, most often a one-carat purest white diamond—"D flawless" as defined by the GIA. Less than two years ago, that investment-grade diamond would have cost about $60,000. At this writing its price has slipped to about $15,000, and by all odds will go still lower. As bank interest rates went higher and higher, diamond investors, who get no interest on their purchase, decided to sell in droves—and suddenly the market that De Beers had so rigidly guarded became flooded with diamonds.

Does that mean that diamonds will lose their value and become as inexpensive as semiprecious stones? Not likely. What will probably happen is what happened to silver a few years ago. After the manipulation of Bunker Hunt, who tried to drive up the price of silver by buying everything available, and actually managed to push silver from about $4 per ounce to an incredible $65, sanity eventually reasserted itself. Hunt, unable to gobble up all the silver in the world and faced with uncomfortable legal and government questions, slunk back to Texas—and silver prices dipped gracefully down to about $6 an ounce (at this writing). Chances are that diamonds, which have been popular for so long and have real beauty and fascination aside from the artificial hype that has accompanied them, will stabilize too at a level close to and perhaps slightly below that of rubies, sapphires and emeralds.

The one fly in the ointment is the proliferation of expert reproductions that have also flooded the market in recent years and taken some of the dollars that would ordinarily have been used for the real thing. There have been counterfeit diamonds almost as long as diamonds have been popular, but up until a few years ago most of them lacked the diamond's fire and were so much softer that they couldn't really pass close inspection. However, with the advent five or six years ago of *cubic zirconium*, a man-made substance with diamantine brilliance and a hardness of about 8, the diamond now has a twin that has fooled many knowledgeable people. You can buy a "flawless" one-carat stone for perhaps a twentieth of the cost of a comparable diamond, and, if the cubic zirconium begins to show signs of wear, it can be easily replaced with another. Why then should anybody buy diamonds? I guess the answer is, "Because they *are* diamonds," because they are natural, unique, dazzlingly beautiful, unchanging—and if their dollar value is a bit unpredictable at present, the pleasure they give and the sentiment they embody is as constant as ever.

How can you tell a real diamond from a fake? The ultimate way is to send it to a lapidary or the GIA. But there are many tests you can do yourself if you suspect that the stone you are being shown is not really genuine.

First of all, diamonds rate 10 on the hardness scale, and are 140 times as hard as the next hardest gems, rubies and sapphires, which rate 9. A diamond will scratch any other gemstone, and will certainly leave a scar on any imitation, but that's not always a safe test. First of all, the owner of the pretender may not be pleased to have you scoring up his stone just to prove your point. Secondly, a modern cut diamond doesn't usually have a sharp enough edge to make such scoring easy. But finally, you will remember I told you that diamonds, though exceedingly hard, can *fracture*. Because of their strong crystalline structure, they will chip readily, and in the effort to scratch a softer stone, you may spoil your own. So unless you have a diamond scriber, or some other kind of diamond needle, don't risk marring a good stone just to prove another one is bad.

Clear quartz crystals (hardness 7) and *paste*, or glass (about 5½) are sometimes mistaken for diamonds, but they lack the diamond's characteristic life and fire. Crystal was often mounted in antique jewelry (in a closed-back, foiled setting) for memorial jewelry, to indicate the purity of the loved one who died, or to serve as a symbol of tears. But diamonds were seldom used in this way. Because diamonds are so hard and so dense, a tiny drop of water will stand up on the surface of a diamond as though the stone were waxed, but on glass or softer stones, it will spread out. If your stone is large enough, this simple and reliable test will help you determine if your stone is a real diamond or glass. Actually, this water test will work for all the precious gemstones, as will another easy method: touch your tongue to the table of the the stone. Diamonds and gemstones are noticeably cold; glass and soft stones are much warmer. But when you test this way, make sure the stone has been sitting alone for a few minutes; any gem that is in contact with your skin, no matter how large, will warm up and invalidate the tongue test.

Let me digress for just a moment and print the Mohs scale out for you. It is a simple and clever arranging of minerals in their order of hardness, though it doesn't indicate how much harder one is than another. The scale is named for its inventor, Friedrich Mohs, who devised it in 1822. It ranks the substances as follows:

1. Talc
2. Gypsum
3. Calcite
4. Fluorspar
5. Apatite
6. Feldspar
7. Quartz
8. Topaz
9. Corundum (ruby, sapphire)
10. Diamond

The principle of the scale is that anything with a higher number can scratch anything of a lower number.

My own thumbnail version of the Mohs scale is even simpler: ordinary blackboard chalk is softest, at 1. Your fingernail (or mine) is about 2½. A copper penny is 3 (they will soon be collectibles, and we'll have to find another substitute, but until we do...). A knife blade is about 5½, as is glass, and a steel file is 6–7. Ordinary kitchen cleansers will scratch anything softer than about 5. It is not a good idea to try to identify any gemstone by scratching it—it is too dangerous, as one substance will undoubtedly get marred by another. But the Mohs scale reliably measures the relative hardness of familiar substances, and helps you to identify them.

All fake diamonds are softer than the real thing, and therefore more subject to wear, less cold to the touch, less likely to cause water to bead up on their surface. Another unique quality of real diamonds is their affinity for grease, probably also a result of their denseness and coldness. Whatever the reason, this particular characteristic is used to separate them from their matrix rock in diamond mines.

It also explains why diamonds have to be cleaned so often and are easily coated with soap or film; take them off before you wash your greasy dishes!

White sapphires, both synthetic and natural, have often been confused with diamonds, and during the Depression the less expensive white sapphires were sometimes substituted for diamonds in engagement rings. These were what have been called "Depression diamonds."

Zircons have intense fiery dispersion, like diamonds, but their hardness is only 7½. Zircons are strongly doubly refractive. Diamonds are singly refractive. If you see a good-sized stone that you suspect may be a zircon and it has an à jour setting (open back) or is loose, use this test: look through the stone at a black pencil line or the edge of a piece of paper, or even the edge of one of its own facets. If you see two lines, the stone is doubly refractive. If you see one line, it is singly refractive.

There are really no other clear, natural stones that closely resemble diamonds, but ingenious man has created a few that might fool you. There is, as I've mentioned, cubic zirconium, or CZ, but its giveaway is its softness; if a diamondlike stone shows any wear along the edges of the facets or on the table (this does not include chipping), it is not a diamond. CZ is absolutely free of flaws or inclusions. But while some diamonds are graded "flawless," it is really a very rare occurrence. The test for a flawless stone is a 10-power loupe, which will usually reveal some signs, no matter how minute, of nature's imperfect role in forming the stone. So, if you see a stone under the microscope and it is absolutely clean and clear, be wary. Either it is a magnificent, rare, perfectly clear diamond...or a phony.

Cubic zirconium does have the fire and requisite clear white color of a good diamond. But it is somewhat heavier, making a one-carat CZ stone slightly smaller in diameter than a one-carat real diamond. But it is difficult to test the size of the stones with accuracy, since both are only about a quarter of an inch across.

Other synthetic materials used to simulate diamonds are strontium titanate, marketed under the name Fabulite, and synthetic rutile, known as Titania. These frankly fake stones have *too much* fire to be diamonds; Fabulite about four times and Titania about six times as much as a real stone. Fabulite is much heavier than diamond, and Titania is yellowish in color, with strong double refraction. One of the more convincing diamond phonies is the diamond doublet—a thin sliver of diamond glued to a worthless colorless base. If you look at this misfit from the side you can see a shadow, and sometimes you can even see glue on the outside edges (use your loupe). In general, be suspicious of any stone that is set deep into a setting, especially if the back is closed, not because good gems are never set that way (they sometimes are), but because the stones are not open to careful inspection, which may mean someone is trying to keep a secret somewhere in that stone.

For many years people believed that no one would ever make a synthetic diamond that could pass muster. By synthetic I mean a man-made stone which is actually of the same chemical composition as a real diamond, not a total phony, like a doublet or a CZ. But in 1955 General Electric announced that it had succeeded in synthesizing diamonds by simulating the natural birth of the gem: subjecting carbonaceous material to extreme pressure and heat. At first these man-made diamonds were too small and too dark to amount to much, but as the work proceeded, the quality of these diamonds improved and the recent stones really do rival natural diamonds; they would be very hard for even the experts to distinguish. Luckily, these man-made diamonds are still quite small, and the complicated procedures necessary to form them make them prohibitively expensive—much more expensive than real, natural ones. However, it is certainly conceivable that in the future GE diamonds will be a whole new category of stones to reckon with.

As with other gemstones, color, clarity and cut determine the value of a diamond. But the criteria for diamonds are much more standardized than those for the other stones. In America, this can be attributed to the work of the GIA, or the Gemological Institute of America. This group has created a strict scale of values that defines exactly what is most desirable in a diamond. Any diamond taken to GIA is thoroughly examined and accompanied by a report that clearly indicates each important feature of the stone and how it ranks. The only information that is not given is the appraised value.

The GIA report begins with a description of the stone, its measurement in millimeters, its carat weight and the shape and style of cut. The description might read something like this:

SHAPE AND CUT: round brilliant
MEASUREMENTS: 6.37–6.41 × 3.97 MM
WEIGHT: 1.06 carats

These measurements are very accurate and precise.

The next phase of a typical GIA report gives the exact proportions of the stone and the cut, and comments on the symmetry and the polish. The same report might continue this way:

PROPORTIONS:

Depth: 62.1%
Table: 60%
Girdle: medium—sl. thick, faceted
Culet: small

FINISH:

Polish:	Good
Symmetry:	Good

There would also be an accompanying diagram, showing the facets above and below the girdle.

Then the report would judge the stone's clarity, taking into account the number, size, placement and nature of any inclusions or surface irregularities. Two to four people give independent opinions on the grading and the diamond is examined under a special binocular microscope. The possible gradings are FLAWLESS, which means the stone receives the highest marks possible: *no* internal or external flaws are visible under magnification; VVS_1, VVS_2, SI, VS_1, VS_2, SI_1, SI_2, I_1, I_2, I_3 and l_3. At the very low end of the scale, the stone is badly marred by flaws, and in all cases, when a stone is judged less than flawless, the flaws are described and their exact positions marked on the diagram.

The diamond's color is judged on a scale that goes from D (the first water, absolutely colorless) to the end of the alphabet, Z (almost yellow). These judgments are not merely subjective; the GIA has a series of diamonds with established color grades against which the stone being studied is judged. Another factor in the judging of color is the amount of fluorescence. Many diamonds do fluoresce (this is sometimes a key to where they come from), and while fluorescence in itself is not the only trait upon which to judge the stone's merit, stones with a strong blue fluorescence generally are not considered to be as valuable as those whose bluish gleam doesn't depend on their reaction to ultraviolet light. A stone may fluoresce other colors, too, but the reaction has to be very strong to affect its color in daylight.

In a section on the report reserved for miscellaneous comments, the GIA "doctors" might include details like "lightly bearded girdle," or "crown angles are greater than 35 degrees" (not perfect proportions), or "significant graining is present." At least three signatures will appear on the report, as well as a file number assuring you that your diamond, once it has undergone this testing, is on file forever in the GIA offices. If it is ever sold or—perish the thought—if it is ever stolen, these permanent records can be invaluable.

For any major colored stone, a GIA report is well worth its modest price. But for a diamond, I feel this report is a *must*. In addition to grading color and clarity, "fingerprinting" your stone in this way makes identification accurate and easy, giving you the benefit of intricate equipment and expert judgment, as well as telling you things you would have a hard time finding out from other sources. For instance, severely flawed diamonds are sometimes subjected to laser beams which will actually burn out a black flaw and leave a white, or barely noticeable, "hole." Even the best-intentioned jeweler might loupe the stone and not see these holes; but the GIA will point them out and locate them for you. Many diamonds, particularly *fancy* (colored) diamonds, have been irradiated or treated to enhance the color. Most of these methods defy detection except by the most advanced instruments. The GIA report will tell you whether your stone has been treated or if its color is natural. Of course it goes without saying that if the stone you bring in for evaluation turns out *not* to be a diamond, the GIA will tell you that, too.

In short, when making an investment in a piece of jewelry, you owe it to yourself to get the best advice possible. A GIA certificate and an independent appraisal (independent of the dealer you are buying from, that is) of its *true market value* are essential. Tell the appraiser you want this since an appraisal for insurance would probably be raised to reflect the fact that your policy might only pay 80 percent of the full market value should the piece be stolen or lost. Also, the expectation is that prices, and hence values, will continue to go up, so that, should you have a loss in the future, your appraisal should still bear some relationship to reality. Your jeweler should also give you a sales slip listing all the important aspects of the stone or piece of jewelry: the stone's size in millimeters, its proportions and weight in carats (only in the case of a large stone, but even a small stone or group of stones should have a carat weight specified on the sales slip), the karat of gold (if there is any), or the identification of any other metal (platinum, white gold, etc.), the price you pay, including the tax, and a clear identification of the stone, e.g., "genuine natural diamond," together with its GIA classification, e.g., "D Flawless." This sales slip is your certification in writing that what the jeweler told you is true, and as such, is like a contract: keep it in a safe place, and if you ever find out that any of the information on it is false, you have a right to demand that the jeweler make restitution to you. A GIA certificate is invaluable in this case, because the diamond you bring back will be clearly fingerprinted as the diamond you bought. In the case of theft, the same would be true.

But as important as it is, a jeweler's sales slip is *not* an appraisal, even though your jeweler may call it that, and most insurance companies will not accept it as one. They know that these sales slips can be inflated if the customer and the salesman agree to do so, and once a piece of jewelry has vanished, an insurance company has no way of ascertaining the exact value of the lost treasure if there is no independent, impartial record.

Perhaps now a word about insurance would be helpful. Most homeowners or personal possessions policies have a very low maximum when it comes to lost, stolen or destroyed jewelry—somewhere in the neighborhood of $500. This is clearly inadequate coverage for any major piece, so if you want to expand your coverage to include diamonds and other precious stones, your insurance agent will probably ask you to list all your major pieces, their value, recent appraisals of them, together with photographs or clear descriptions, and add all the valuations together. He will then write a special rider to cover them, and charge you about 16 percent of the value of the jewelry as each year's premium.

I know people who, when they take their jewelry out of the vault, get special one-night policies that cost anywhere from $50 to $500, just for the privilege of wearing their own beautiful things. And I have other friends who get their lovely, genuine pieces copied, so that if they lose or break them, or if they are stolen, the real jewels will lie safe in the vault, untouched. More than one jewelry owner keeps all the "good stuff" in the bank and wears costume jewelry. Why even own the jewelry, you may wonder, if you can't enjoy wearing it? My own feeling is that paying high insurance premiums for the privilege of wearing your own possessions ultimately takes all the pleasure out of owning them. In fact, to me jewelry is so personal and special a belonging that even if I recovered three times its value, I would still feel that nothing could replace it. So I'd rather keep the money others pay for premiums, and buy more jewelry. And I do wear mine—but only a little at a time; the rest stays safely in the vault. I treasure it and take care of it, and when I travel, never leave it in luggage or in a hotel room; anybody who steals it will have to take me along with it! And I've promised myself—and I hope I'll have the stoutness of heart to keep this promise—that if something I love is ever lost, stolen or broken, I won't shed a single tear. I'll remember it as I would an old dear friend, with pleasure and without regret. That's what jewelry is all about to me: beauty and pleasure, not just dollars and investment.

I'm simply passing on my philosophy; many other jewelry lovers feel differently. What I *am* recommending is that you know as much about your jewelry as you possibly can—including what will happen if it is lost, damaged or stolen.

One more word about diamonds. My own preference is for fancy diamonds, and I have watched them steadily increase in value over the years. For the purists who believe "diamond" means "pure colorless diamond," fancies may have no appeal, but if you've ever seen their rich color *plus* the fire in their depths, I think you would be hard put to dismiss them. By "fancy" I don't mean yellowish but a full-out canary yellow diamond; not pinkish, or greenish or bluish but strong pink, green or blue. Fancies are sufficiently rare, so their prices are consistently high, and my guess is that all the irradiating and dyeing and processing will not change their strong upward growth. In fact, with the current turbulence in the price of investment grade diamonds, fancies may even forge ahead. If you see one and fall in love with it, and are lucky enough to be able to buy it (after a thorough GIA testing assures you that it is genuine), I think you will have a "best buy." My own favorite piece of jewelry is an opalescent marquise-shaped fancy, set into a twenties platinum ring that surrounds it with tiny brilliants and black enamel. The diamond is really more "moony" than opalescent, but it is truly a beautiful and unusual stone. I have never seen one quite like it, and if you have, I hope you will write to me about it.

Diamonds are the birthstone for April.

The Semiprecious
Stones

The term "semiprecious" stone is in a way a misleading one, because it implies that anything in this
broad category, which includes turquoise, garnet, topaz,
zircon, amethyst, carnelian—*any* stone, in fact, that has
some value but isn't one of the Big Four—is less valuable
than a "precious" stone. In fact, this isn't true. A truly fine
aquamarine or topaz or tourmaline can be worth much
more than a poor quality ruby or emerald. Just as with the
precious stones, clarity (where it applies), cut (where it
applies), color, size and even history will contribute to the
value of a semiprecious stone. Let's look, then, at some of
the so-called semiprecious stones, and you will see how
varied they really are.

None of these stones is as hard as the precious gems,
but some are certainly hard enough to make fine centers
for jewelry and rings. Some are rather soft, like turquoise
and lapis lazuli, some are faceted and fiery as diamonds,
some are usually cut cabochon (with rounded tops and flat
bottoms), some are clear, some opaque, some cloudy with
inclusions. And some materials—like amber and coral—
really aren't stones or gems at all, but because of their
beauty and rarity and their use in jewelry are also usually
classified as semiprecious stones. Perhaps, then, the best

way to approach them is simply to discuss them in alphabetical order:

AGATE

Agate is a type of quartz, a common stone that is often quite beautiful. It appears in a variety of patterns: with stripes, it is called *banded agate*, when black it is called *onyx*, when it has markings that look like little trees or plants it is known as *moss* or *dendritic agate*. Agates come in many colors, one of which is the common orange red of *carnelian*, often used for seals or signet rings.

Agate is an ancient material. Agate beads and jewelry were traded by merchants in the Middle East as early as the fifth century B.C. Egyptians, Greeks and Romans appreciated and used it too; I have a tiny Roman gold ring with an agate oval featuring a carved fertility symbol: the sex organs of a man. Museums contain many fine examples of agate seals, carved backwards and in intaglio, so that their owners could press them into clay and use them as signatures; agate is hard and cold, so it doesn't stick to clay or wax.

Eye agate was often used for magical beads in ancient times, and many *stone cameos* were carved out of banded agate. These cameos of stone are generally valued more highly than the more common (and more easily carved) shell variety.

Agates were valued as charms against danger in earlier times, and are still worn as talismans in eastern countries. The owner of an Afghanistan shop, a man I know who specializes in beads and jewelry, once showed me some agates that were supposed to cure earache in his country. I wouldn't guarantee the earache cure—nor would he!— but the beads were beautifully fashioned and of fine color. Indian agate beads, known as beggar beads, and consisting of multicolored stones of different shapes, are popular today, and some of them are quite fascinating, though rather heavy to wear.

The nineteenth-century Victorians always liked agate. They used it in rings, necklaces, earrings, pins (or "brooches") and bracelets, and their Scotch agate jewelry, which usually features a number of different colored agate stones carefully set into silver, is still sought-after today.

Agates are often dyed to intensify their color, but this doesn't really affect their value. They are hard (Mohs scale: 7) but easily chipped, and they take a fine polish, or they can be tumbled into baroque shapes that are quite attractive. No two are ever alike in size or markings, and rock shops and hobbyists use many of these stones.

Most agate mined today comes from India or Brazil, but it occurs naturally all over the world.

You can distinguish agate from glass, which it sometimes resembles, by its greater coldness, heaviness and hardness.

ALEXANDRITE

You will probably never see true alexandrite in your lifetime, for it is very rare, but fake alexandrite, usually made of glass or some other substitute, occasionally appears. True alexandrite looks green in daylight and red under artificial light. It is a variety of crysoberyl, and was first discovered in Russia in 1830 on the birthday of Czar Alexander, which accounts for its name. If someone wants to sell you alexandrite, be sure to have it checked by the GIA or a comparable expert before buying.

ALMANDINE GARNET (see *GARNET*)

AMBER

Amber is not actually a stone or gem at all, but the sap from an ancient tree, fossilized and probably washed up on a Baltic shore. Very often amber contains trapped bits of leaf or long-dead insects, and these pieces are especially prized. Amber is soft and light and warm to the touch. Rub it hard against wool or the hair on your head, and it will "electrify," picking up tiny bits of paper. This is one of the ways of identifying it. However, there are certain kinds of plastics resembling amber which also have this property, so this isn't a definitive test. True amber has a resinous smell, and if you prick it with a hot needle, or even warm it swiftly with the friction of your hands, that fragrance will identify it. It also floats in water and sinks in brine, and has a distinctive "fat," rather waxy or sticky feel.

Amber can be cloudy or clear, and comes in a variety of different colors. The most common is a golden yellow, but you will also see it in red (*cherry amber*), orange, reddish orange (*tomato amber*), brown, black (sometimes confused with *jet*, which is very similar), or, rarely, white, blue or green.

Amber has been used for jewelry since earliest times, and was believed to have magical properties even as late as the nineteenth century, when it was burned in sickrooms to "purify" the air. Amber beads were an important item of trade in the centuries before Christ, and are still highly valued in Middle East countries, in Africa, and in the Baltic countries where much of it originates. The Chinese, too, liked amber, particularly clear, red amber, carving it over the centuries into lovely snuffboxes and pipestems.

In the nineteenth century amber beads were often faceted beautifully, but today most amber beads are crudely polished into clumsy "baroque" shapes and, to my eye, are not very attractive. *Ambroid* (pressed or powdered amber) and *copal* (a similar, but not as valuable resinous substance, always uniformly cloudy, never clear or layered) are often passed off as amber, but they are not the same thing. Plastic "amber" has been made for a long time, and some of it is good enough to fool the experts. The smell and feel test, in addition to the fact that plastic, when heated, gives off an unpleasant odor, should give away an imposter. Also the plastic amber, if it is clear, is not as interesting and varied as true amber; it is usually uniform in color, and the "inclusions" are specks or fake bugs without the range and surprise of true amber. Another test: true amber fluoresces slightly to a rather whitish yellow under black light. And remember, heat and acids damage amber; put on your perfume and hairspray before your beads. If amber gets gummy or dirty, simple soap and water, or a quick wipe with a soft cloth and alcohol should clean it off nicely.

AMETHYST

Amethyst is a beautiful purple quartz that has been prized from earliest times. When it is clear, sparkling and well-cut it really deserves its classification as a gemstone. It is strongly dichroic, and in good amethysts, definite blue purple and red purple colors are visible. Fine amethysts come from Brazil, and the older Siberian amethysts from Russia can be extraordinarily dark and rich in color. We have amethysts in this country, too; I have dug them up myself from old quarries around Paterson, New Jersey, and found them in geodes (nodules of crystals trapped in a potato-shaped rock) in the Midwest. Amethysts can also be found in Uruguay, Ceylon, India, Madagascar and South Africa.

Amethysts were believed to protect their wearers against being wounded in battle, to sharpen their wits and keep them from being poisoned. The most common folklore held that it would prevent drunkenness; hence, the name, *amethystos*, in Greek, meaning "not drunk."

Amethyst is seldom imitated because it is quite inexpensive, but its beauty makes its value far exceed its monetary worth. It is the birthstone for February.

AQUAMARINE

Like amethyst, aquamarine's beauty equals that of much more costly stones, but because it is fairly common, occurring frequently in large, clear crystals, its price is comparatively modest. The best color for aquamarine is a rich transparent blue green, rather like the Mediterranean Sea. Large aquamarines are often square cut to show off their intense clarity and striking color.

Aquamarine is a kind of beryl, identical in chemical composition and hardness (7½–8) to its more highly prized, rarer cousin, emerald. Like emerald, too, aquamarine is dichroic, the colors being bluish green and clear, or "white." Aquamarines are often heat-treated to intensify their blue color, a treatment whose results will not fade or change over the years. Aquamarine is the birthstone for March.

AVENTURINE

Not exactly a semiprecious stone, aventurine is more often used in costume jewelry. It is a very pretty, bronze-spangled *feldspar*, which is sometimes called *sunstone*. It is similar to—but not the same as—*aventurine quartz*, which is spangled with mica flakes, or *aventurine glass*, sometimes called *goldstone*, which is merely imitation aventurine.

You can tell the difference between the three stones by their hardness: feldspar is about 6, quartz about 7 and glass only about 5½.

BLOODSTONE

Bloodstone, known in early times as *heliotrope*, is a type of noncrystalline quartz, usually dark green or blackish in color, with small red dots resembling drops of blood. It is often used in seals and signet rings, and sometimes as part of the beggar beads from India. It is an alternate birthstone for March.

BRAZILIANITE

This is a yellowish green stone first found in Brazil in 1944 in the Minas Gerais mines, and later in New Hampshire. The crystals are rather large but soft (Mohs scale: 5½) and have not been used much for jewelry.

CARNELIAN (see AGATE)

CAT'S EYE

A yellowish brown form of crysoberyl, this stone, when cut in a cabochon (round on top, flat on the bottom) shows a silky, moving flash of light called *chatoyancy*. The effect is similar to that of the "star" in a star ruby or sapphire. Other stones, like tiger's eye, or some forms of quartz or tourmaline, show this chatoyancy, but only true cat's eye has a milky opalescence as well, which really does look like the staring eye of a cat. Cat's eye is occasionally used in men's rings; it was more popular at the turn of the century, when shimmer or opalescence in any form was very much in vogue. Most cat's eyes come from Ceylon.

CRYSOCOLLA

This blue or bluish green opaque stone is sometimes confused with turquoise. It is very soft (2–4 on the Mohs scale) and is usually found in association with copper, and is polished *en cabochon*.

CHRYSOPRASE

An apple-green translucent quartz, chrysoprase is sometimes used for beads or cameos. It comes from Australia and Brazil, and, since it is listed in the Bible as one of the foundations of the New Jerusalem, must have been mined in the Near East at some time.

CORAL

Coral is neither a gem nor a stone, but I'm including it here because, as a component of jewelry, its value and popularity are comparable to that of the semiprecious stones we've been discussing. Coral is actually the skeleton of a sea creature, the coral polyp. The red, or *noble coral* has been popular as jewelry since ancient times, and other varieties, notably white and *angel skin*, or light pink, are also highly valued. Coral takes a beautiful polish, and cut into beads or cameos, it makes a handsome adornment. The Victorian belief that coral beads protected against sore throats and quinsy prompted many anxious mothers to place a tiny necklace of coral around their babies' necks. Another legend told of coral's ability to change color with a woman's menstrual cycle. In many primitive societies, a man's worth is measured by his wife's jewelry, and coral, ivory, coins, silver, amber, lapis and turquoise are among the most desirable materials.

The finest red coral today comes from the Italian coast, and the most skilled coral carvers are the Italians, though the Chinese in particular have been responsible over the years for beautiful coral work. Strands of *branch coral* are also strung uncut to make spiky, attractive necklaces, and black and blue coral, though less highly valued, has been made into interesting jewelry. White coral is often dyed to enhance color, natural coral of good color is the most desirable and the larger the beads and the finer the carving, the more you can expect to pay.

Fake coral is often made from glass or plastic, but it is easy to spot. A drop of lemon juice or any weak acid will effervesce on coral, which is composed of calcium carbonate. If you look through a magnifying glass you can easily see the bubbles. Glass or plastic will be untouched by lemon juice or acid. Also, real coral is relatively soft (Mohs scale: 3) and can be scratched with the blade of a knife.

CRYSTAL (see ROCK CRYSTAL)

DEMANTOID (see GARNET)

GARNET

Garnets have everything going for them as gemstones—beauty, hardness, variety, color—but they are extremely plentiful, and therefore, in our supply-and-demand society, grossly undervalued. Perhaps they also suffer from reverse snobbism, as they were once very popular with the lower classes and in "peasant" jewelry, particularly the red variety, known as *Bohemian garnets* but properly called *pyrope*.

These red garnets can have a marvelous pigeon blood color rivaling that of the best rubies (though they are not dichroic, and therefore lack the play of colors rubies have). Now they are usually showily faceted, though in the past they were often cut as cabochons. This made them look like a beautiful jellied candy or a drop of blood; they were called *carbuncles*.

Perhaps the most popular color for garnets, though not the most common, is the purplish red variety known as *almandine*. Green garnets, called *demantoids*, are extremely rare (consequently expensive!) and have a fire and life equal to diamonds. Their green color is less dark and "blue" than emeralds, less "yellow" than peridots; it is a grass green brightness that is most like green fancy diamonds; once seen, it is not forgotten.

Demantoids, too, were once more popular in Victorian

jewelry, though they were never common, and stones of large size were very seldom seen. Now, however, they are virtually unobtainable.

There are other varieties of garnets, but they are scarcely ever seen in jewelry. Garnet is the birthstone for January. Like amethyst, garnet is seldom imitated because the original is so inexpensive and easy to get. (Garnets are found all over—even in Central Park!) But they are occasionally faked with glass, which is much softer and much warmer to the touch.

HEMATITE

A rarely used brilliant blue black stone with iron oxide as its main ingredient, hematite is sometimes used for seals or signets, or occasionally for beads, though it was more popular for all these uses a century ago. Most hematite is mined in England and cut in Germany. When you rub hematite on a stone, it leaves a red mark, like rust.

HELIODOR

Another variety of beryl, this one golden yellow, which is sometimes used in jewelry. "Heliodor" means "gift of the sun." It is found in Brazil, Madagascar and Southwest Africa. Some crystals have a small amount of uranium, and are radioactive.

HELIOTROPE

This is another name for bloodstone.

HYACINTH

This name is usually given to orange red zircons, or sometimes to similarly colored (grossular) garnets. In the Bible,

Cultured Freshwater Pearls

Two types of cultured fresh water pearls from Lake Biwa, Japan: large baroques and rounds. —Photo courtesy Gemological Institute of America

Natural Ruby Crystals

Natural ruby crystals in matrix show the crystalline structure and fine red color. —Photo courtesy Gemological Institute of America

Which is the Real Diamond?

A read-through test combs out "synthetics." Table down, the real diamond (right) will not read through; YAG (left) and CZ (middle) will.
—Photo courtesy Gemological Institute of America

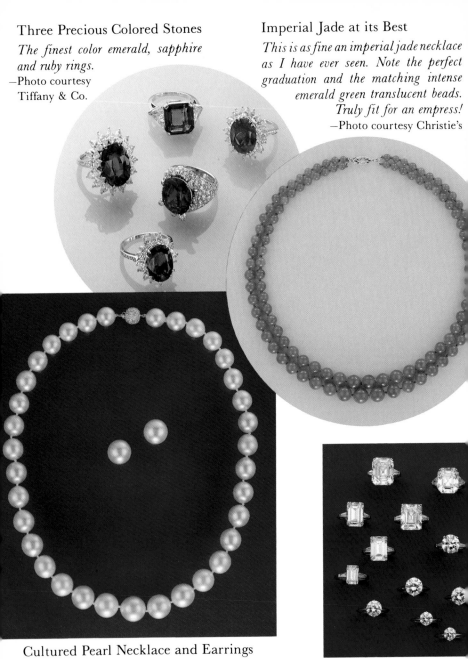

Three Precious Colored Stones

The finest color emerald, sapphire and ruby rings.

—Photo courtesy Tiffany & Co.

Imperial Jade at its Best

This is as fine an imperial jade necklace as I have ever seen. Note the perfect graduation and the matching intense emerald green translucent beads. Truly fit for an empress!

—Photo courtesy Christie's

Cultured Pearl Necklace and Earrings

This magnificent pearl set is of finest color and rosee. The thirty-five pearls are slightly graduated, from 11.5 to 15 mm. The earrings are matched button pearls, measuring about 13.15 x 14.65 mm. —Photo courtesy Christie's

Solitaire Diamond Ring in the Most Popular Tiffany Cuts

Rubies in All Their Glory

This magnificent ruby and diamond necklace once belonged to screen star Merle Oberon and sold at auction for $100,000. Rubies are in cabochon and oval cuts, diamonds in squares, rounds and baguettes—all set in platinum. —Photo courtesy Christie's

Yellow Fancy Diamond

This striking "fancy" is rare and spectacular. Each one has a GIA "pedigree" that certifies it is "of natural color." This yellow fancy weighs about seven carats. —Photo courtesy Christie's

Emerald-cut, marquise-shaped, pear-shaped and round brilliant-cut.
—Photo courtesy Tiffany & Co.

A Rainbow of Sapphire Colors

Angela Cummings of Tiffany's designed this brilliant necklace with forty-nine pastel sapphires and over 1000 diamonds set in platinum.
—Photo courtesy Tiffany & Co.

Chains of Various Links

An interesting collection of gold chains. From outside to inside they are: curve link, filed curb link, filed cable link, rope chain and foxtail. —Photo courtesy Tiffany & Co.

Multicolored Gold

This beautiful necklace designed by Angela Cummings uses three colors of gold—red, yellow and green—plus copper to depict fall leaves.
—Photo courtesy Tiffany & Co.

though, "jacinth" or "hyacinth" referred to a blue stone, probably our present-day sapphire.

IVORY

Like coral and amber, ivory is neither a stone nor a gem. It comes from the tusks of living elephants if it is elephant ivory, the finest variety, or, if it is the less valuable kind, from the nuts or seeds of certain trees. Bone, which is often confused with ivory, and is similar in its working qualities, is also used for jewelry, as are various other tooth and tusk materials. But elephant ivory, with its rich, fatty luster and myriad of fine crosshatchings has a beauty, a workability and a value unlike that of any other ivory. It has been used for jewelry since time began, and is still prized, though many countries, including our own, have laws restricting the importation of ivory because of the cruelty to an endangered species that securing it often entails.

The finest ivory is as sleek and rich-looking as cream, and when it ages, it takes on a beautiful tan color. Extremely popular lately are old Indian ivory bracelets, thick cuffs with silver clasps and red dye to enhance the natural markings. Also popular is carved whale ivory, called scrimshaw, which has been part of our history since the old whaling days. Many beautiful ivory beads are imported, too, or are still around from our grandmothers' days, when ivory was a favorite material for jewelry.

Bone is very similar in appearance to ivory, but instead of the crosshatching, bone shows a straight grain, which looks almost like little stitches, along its length, and when it ages it turns a yellowish color rather than rich brown. (This effect is sometimes faked by soaking new pieces of bone or vegetable ivory in strong tea. Watch out!) Bone doesn't have the luster ivory comes by naturally, but age, the oil from skin or even wax can make it look more "fatty" than it would without the enhancement.

Cheaper jewelry from Oriental or primitive countries is often made of bone or vegetable ivory. There is nothing intrinsically wrong with either material, as long as it isn't being passed off as something it's not. Usually the carving on bone or vegetable ivory, because the materials are less valued, are less expert, which may be another way of telling it from real elephant ivory. The ivory the Eskimos use for their interesting and valuable carving is usually walrus ivory, sometimes ancient pieces that were used as tent pegs and later abandoned or buried; these become fossilized and take on a typical spongelike appearance that is prized.

Ivory can last a long time if you take care of it. It should never be subjected to soaking. If it becomes soiled, a wipe with a damp soapy cloth, or sometimes a bit of baby oil, will do the trick. Never let it become too hot or too cold. Obviously you wouldn't put ivory jewelry in the refrigerator, but leaving it in a cold—or hot—car could be equally devastating. Sunlight will actually bleach ivory, so if you don't like the soft mellow patina it develops you could put it out on a sunny day (being careful not to let it heat up too much) to lighten it.

In all its forms, ivory will fluoresce whitish under the black light, but the plastic "ivory," which sometimes looks so much like it, will not, so that's one way of telling the difference. Plastic is usually lighter, too, and can never quite duplicate either nature's crosshatching of true ivory or its fat, buttery luster. If you train yourself, you will seldom be fooled.

JADE

Because the term "semiprecious stone" has become an imprecise catch-all, I'm including jade in the category, although I think—and many experts will agree—that jade is not only precious, but, like pearls, in a class all by itself.

There are two main types of jade. *Nephrite jade*, a greasy-looking opaque or semitranslucent stone, doesn't usually take a high polish, and comes in soft colors like gray, grayish green, brown, white or yellowish brown. This was the stone used for all the ancient jade pieces, some of which date back to prehistory. Three thousand years ago the Chinese were already carving this nephrite into ornaments and talismans as well as bowls, figures and ceremonial objects. Because jade is tough and tools in those days were so primitive, it sometimes took a lifetime, or even the lifetimes of two or three generations of carvers, to fully execute the work on a single piece of jade. Until modern times this carving was done with stone, wood and bamboo tools charged with sand and water, a tedious, exhausting method. It's hard to believe, when you see the delicacy and joy in piece after piece of jade carving, how much intense effort, time and care went into them.

Nephrite jade is found in various parts of China, and also in New Zealand where it was carved by the Maoris into *tikis* (good-luck figures) as well as weapons and ornaments. It can also be found in Alaska, the United States, Mexico and Poland.

The more valuable kind of jade, called *jadeite*, is brighter in its colors and takes a higher polish. It is jadeite that sometimes occurs in the glorious translucent emerald green called *imperial jade* that can be worth more than the most exquisite diamond. Other jadeite colors are lavender, orange, pink, white and the lovely green flecks on white background which the Chinese call "moss on snow."

Imitations of jade can range from very crude glass phonies to beautifully carved *bowenite*, which is a form of *serpentine* and is imported from China under the name "New Jade." It is softer than real jade, which has a hardness of 6½ (nephrite) or 7 (jadeite), and can be scratched with a knife. Several other soft stones are carved to imitate jade as well, including the yellowish or reddish soapstone so popular with our parents a generation ago.

Real jade is hard, exceedingly tough and cold to the touch. It has a high value, both in the Orient and the United States, and in fact is collected all over the world by experts and jewelry lovers alike. Oriental girls used to wear a jade bracelet from infancy, and as they grew it became impossible to remove. My Chinese friends who share my love of jade tell me that everyone they grew up with had a bit of jade for good luck, even if it was just a "fingering piece," and that they loved to study the symbols carved in jade, each one of which had its own special meaning, and to collect the many colors. My friends tell me, too, that jade "changes" as it is worn, as pearls do, and that the colors get brighter and clearer when you are in good health. This is said to be especially true of the imperial green color, and I have seen these changes in jade I own and wear next to my skin. This "living" quality of jade makes it particularly personal and interesting to own and wear. Incidentally, no jadeite, also called "Chinese jade," actually comes from China. It was first imported to China from Burma, where it principally originates, during the seventeenth century. Therefore, no jadeite piece is "ancient" or "primitive." Don't let a dealer tell you it is!

JASPER

This is a kind of opaque quartz stone, usually red or brown, that is sometimes set into rings or seals. Petrified wood is a variety of jasper.

JET

You will not see any real jet in modern jewelry, because it is no longer being mined. But jet, which is a hard glossy peatlike material that looks surprisingly like coal, was very popular in Victorian times as a material for mourning jewelry. Nowadays what might be sold to you as jet probably refers to the color, and is likely to be made of glass, plastic or—if you're lucky—onyx.

KUNZITE

One of the few "new" gemstones, kunzite was first discovered in San Diego County, California, around the turn of the century. It is a very pretty violet or pink violet stone in the *spodumene* family, and though hard to cut, makes a very lively gem. It can also be found in Brazil and Madagascar.

KYANITE

Also known as *disthene*, kyanite is a rare and lively blue stone resembling sapphire or sometimes aquamarine. Occasionally kyanite cat's eyes (q.v.) are found, but these are quite rare. Kyanite is one of the few stones that is multicolored, or *pleochroic*: in this case, the colors are white (clear), blue violet and cobalt.

LAPIS LAZULI

Lapis lazuli, like turquoise, is not translucent but opaque, meaning that you cannot see light through it. It is massy rather than crystalline, and so it is very seldom cut in facets, but nearly always in cabochons, rounds or beads. The best lapis is a beautiful dark clear blue, sometimes flecked with a substance that looks like gold, but is really pyrite. Lapis of lesser quality is lighter and often streaked with gray, but if there is white present, and no flecks, the stone is probably *sodalite*, which is often passed off as true lapis, but definitely isn't.

Lapis has been used for jewelry since earliest times, and the Egyptians were especially fond of it. It was also used for many years to make ultramarine blue, a pigment favored by many painters.

In ancient times lapis lazuli was sometimes called sapphire, thereby causing some confusion about which stone is meant when "sapphire" is referred to in the Bible. But since lapis comes from the Middle East, is easy to cut and work, and was most likely used very early, it is generally thought to be the stone referred to in the Bible.

The oldest lapis mines are in Afghanistan, and this country still produces some of the finest stones. This area is still mined and has been in work steadily since before Marco Polo. Lapis is also found in Chile, Colorado, California and Burma. Its hardness on the Mohs scale is 5½–6.

MALACHITE

A banded green stone, malachite is a very handsome copper ore that is often used for jewelry or decorative objects. Malachite beads from Africa have been especially popular lately, and pins with malachite centers were common in the nineteenth century. Small animals and eggs, dishes and cups of malachite were skillfully carved by Russian craftsmen from the fine material mined in the Ural mountains, and nowadays modern versions of these modest treasures are still popular. Today's malachite comes from Australia, the United States, Africa or the Soviet Union.

Though it's not likely that you would mistake anything else for malachite, there have been glass imitations, so if you want to be perfectly sure, simply drop a small bit of hydrochloric acid on your stone. If it is malachite, it will fizz. Be sure to have a paper napkin or other cloth ready to wipe the acid off so that you don't injure the finish of your stone.

MOONSTONE

A whitish or bluish translucent feldspar, the moonstone is always cut cabochon or in rounds to show off its ability to catch the light when moved. It is doubly refractive and rather soft (Mohs scale: 6), and is sometimes mistaken for water opal, which it resembles; however, moonstone doesn't have the "fire" of water opal.

MOSS AGATE (see AGATE)

ONYX (see AGATE)

OPAL

Opal is a beautiful, fiery gemstone, prized for the flash of iridescence that plays across its surface or rests deep in its heart. Opal was known as early as Greek and Roman days, but was particularly popular in Queen Victoria's time, thanks to the Queen herself, who cannily exploited the new, rich discoveries of opal in Australia by wearing the stones and giving them as gifts.

Unlike other gems, opal has no cleavage. It was originally a jellylike substance that was deposited and then hardened in rock seams. There is still a relatively high water content in opal which must be preserved; if the gem is subjected to extreme dryness or heat it will "dry out" and lose its fire. Proper care for these stones includes an occasional long soak in pure water or half-water, half-glycerine. Wearing also improves opal; the heat and oil of your body, combined with the humidity in the air, preserves its fire. But the stone is delicate, rather soft (hardness: 5½–6½) and subject to scratches and cracks. This delicacy is probably the main reason for opal's reputation as a bad-luck stone. Also contributing to this idea is *Anne of Geierstein*, by Sir Walter Scott, a novel widely read in the nineteenth century that features a heroine who comes to grief because of her opals. Plenty of people are unimpressed by opal's frailties and folklore, and it is an extremely popular gem. In fact, it is the birthstone for October.

The four main varieties of opal are *white*, which has a milky white background with flashes of color; *black*, which is really more like deep peacock blue and is the rarest and most expensive; *fire opal*, which is a translucent red or yellowish stone that sometimes lacks fire; and *harlequin*, a variety from Czechoslovakia, which has small points of intense, changeable color. Another, rarer type is *water opal*, which is clear, almost glasslike, with a flash of color.

Today, most opals come from Australia, where they are mined in the center of the country in a desert so hot that the miners have to live underground. All black opal is from Australia. Fire opal is mined in Mexico, and the old Czechoslovakian mines, which are now within the borders of Hungary, still produce beautiful harlequins.

Opals are porous, so if you wash the dishes with your opal ring on it may soak up some of the dirty water. Opals also may shrink slightly when the weather is very cold, so make sure they are tightly held in their settings so they can't slip if they get chilled. All this may seem a lot of trouble to go through for a gemstone, but remember that an opal, cherished and cosseted, can give you many years of pleasure, and like any other "living" thing, repays your care and attention many times over.

It's difficult to imitate an opal, and you probably won't be fooled by the opal glass that occasionally appears masquerading as the real thing. But opal doublets or triplets— a thin slice of real opal glued to a worthless backing to form a doublet or sandwiched between two clear panes of plastic as a triplet—can be mistaken for a solid opal if you're not careful. These doublets and triplets are of little value and their prices should reflect that. Always be suspicious of any opal that has a black underside or, in fact, any stone whose underside isn't visible. And always examine your opal under 10X magnification for wear, chips, cracks or flaws (this is true of any stone, but because opals are so frail it's essential). And always ask: is this a genuine natural opal and not a doublet or triplet?

PEARLS (see *chapter on pearls*)

PERIDOT

A transparent yellowish-green stone, peridot is not as popular today as in the Victorian period, when it was included in so much multicolored jewelry. It is, however, not particularly rare, so its price tag, at least, is popular.

Peridot is rather soft (Mohs scale: 6½) so it tends to show wear in a ring, though it stands up well in pins and pendants. The most valuable color is clear grassy yellow-green; a brownish stone is less valuable. Peridot is doubly refractive and has a characteristic "oily" shine that will help you distinguish it from imposters. In Biblical times, peridot, then called "topaz," was found only near the Red Sea, but now it is chiefly mined in the famous Mogok Stone Tract in Burma, which produces many kinds of gems, as well as in Australia, Norway, Brazil and the United States. Peridot is sometimes called *olivine* or *chrysolite*.

PYROPE (see *GARNET*)

RHINESTONE

A cheap glass imitation diamond, not even deserving to be dignified by the term semiprecious. It would not even appear here at all, except that sometimes dealers in jewelry present rhinestones as though they were stones. Rhinestones can make very pretty costume jewelry and, when well set and well designed can sometimes fool the eye, especially at night. But they are not *real* anything, except real rhinestones!

ROCK CRYSTAL

Clear, colorless quartz. The Greek name for it, *krystallos*, means ice, and that is what it looks like. In the seventeenth and eighteenth centuries it was used for mourning jewelry and for shoe buckles and even more formal adornments, because under candlelight its gleam and glow were somewhat like those of diamonds. The old crystal pieces that were painstakingly cut and fitted into mountings by hand are considered to be treasures today, despite the fact that the crystals themselves do not have much monetary value. In the twenties there was a vogue for long necklaces of crystal beads. Some of these were indeed rock crystal; others were glass. You can easily tell the difference: crystal is cold to the touch (try the tip of your tongue), much harder and doubly refractive. Nowadays crystals are not used much for jewelry, though some designers, like Elsa Peretti of Tiffany's, have discovered it again and carved it into lovely snakes, hearts and zodiac animals.

Rutilated crystal, which has inclusions of long rutile needles and is quite interesting to look at, was popular in pendants a few years ago, and carved crystal seals were once very much desired. Unfortunately, today there are few old craftsmen left with the skill and patience to do the carving. If you buy an uncarved seal in the hope of having it decorated with your own initials, you may search a long time before you will find a willing and able artisan.

Rock crystal, which was also used for the first "crystal balls," was supposed to be a symbol of purity and virginity, and to have the power to bring rain.

ROSE QUARTZ

This is a pink, semitranslucent quartz sometimes used for jewelry. Today rose quartz is usually seen in baroque strands of beads from India and, as is typical of Indian beads, though the material is often beautiful, the beads are often poorly drilled and carelessly faceted or polished. But a generation ago, beautiful rose quartz beads and pendants were carved in China, and if you encounter any of those pieces, the quality will be much, much higher.

Rose quartz, like all quartz, is hard and takes a good polish, but it is not usually very clear. It is massy, not crystalline, and of a pleasant soft pink color, sometimes shading to white. Though it is mined around the world, the best quality rose quartz comes from Brazil.

RUTILATED QUARTZ (see ROCK CRYSTAL)

SARDONYX

Red and white banded chalcedony (massy quartz) usually used for seals or cameos.

SMOKY QUARTZ

This is a brownish clear quartz sometimes used for beads or jewelry.

SODALITE

This is a very pretty blue stone and one of the components in lapis lazuli whose resemblance to that substance is exploited by dealers around the world. Beware. Sodalite never has the gold-colored flecks characteristic of most lapis (though sometimes these flecks are absent in lapis, too), and is usually a somewhat lighter blue, with white areas, while true lapis usually has gray. It is of the same hardness, though, and is similarly used. Sodalite comes from Canada, India, Brazil, Africa and many places in the United States. It is not as valuable as lapis, and should not be sold to you under false pretenses. If you are interested in lapis, practice identifying sodalite and get familiar with the look of both materials so that neither you nor your jewelry dealer will make a mistake.

SPHENE

Sometimes called "titanite," this lively yellow, brown or green stone, though relatively soft (Mohs scale: 5½), has so much fire—actually more than a diamond—that it makes a handsome gemstone. Sphene is mined in Switzerland, the Austrian Tyrols, Canada, California, Brazil and Madagascar.

SPINEL

This pretty red (or blue, or purple) gemstone could easily stand on its own, but its most commonly known characteristic is that it is often mistaken—or substituted—for ruby. The famous Black Prince's Ruby in the British royal regalia is really a spinel, as are several other famous "rubies." In fact, the term "balas ruby" really means spinel.

Actually, spinel and ruby are distantly related, but rubies are harder (Mohs scale: 9) than spinel (Mohs scale: 8) and much richer in color because of their dichroism; spinels are a single shade of red, more like garnets.

Synthetic spinels are often passed off as rubies, sapphires or even diamonds, though they have nothing resembling the fire of a diamond—and spinel itself, even the natural kind, is much less valuable.

Nevertheless spinels are handsome stones in all their

color varieties, and not to be dismissed. They are principally mined in Burma, Thailand, Ceylon, Brazil and Afghanistan.

TANZANITE

A bluish violet transparent stone discovered in Tanzania in 1967. It has a hardness of 6, and occurs in various colors which are usually heat-treated to bring out the characteristic tanzanite blue.

TIGER'S EYE

An interesting brownish gold stone which has a chatoyant luster, like cat's eye or star rubies and sapphires. The chatoyancy is in ribs or stripes, and one unique quality of tiger's eye (sometimes called "tigereye") is that the stripes are reversed as the stone is turned around. Tiger's eye is actually a form of quartz—as so many semiprecious stones are—and the "threads" that form the chatoyant strips are what's left of asbestos, the original material, now decomposed or petrified into quartz material.

Tiger's eye makes attractive beads and inexpensive cabochon jewelry. Most tiger's eye comes from Griqualand West in South Africa.

TOPAZ

Most people think of topaz as the brilliant sherry brown that is the favored color for this beautiful gemstone. But topaz also comes in pink, yellow, blue green (similar to aquamarine), blue, red and "white," or clear. Gem topaz has a hardness of 8, and takes polishing beautifully. However, it does have a tendency to fracture and cause iridescent flaws that spoil its clarity.

Topaz is often confused with *topaz quartz*, a crystalline

quartz stone that is not nearly as valuable or rare as the real thing. The color of topaz quartz is different, too, brownish yellow rather than rich, reddish sherry. Quartz only has a hardness of 7, and does not have the brilliance and luster of true gem topaz.

Another way to tell true topaz from quartz: like amber, topaz is electrified by rubbing against wool or even your own hair, and will pick up small bits of paper. Topaz is also dichroic, and will show two colors; quartz does not.

The most popular topaz color comes only from the mines in Ouro Preto, Brazil, but other colors are mined in Russia, Japan, Australia, Tasmania, the United States, Ceylon and Scotland. Topaz is often heat-treated to improve or deepen its color. It is the birthstone for those born in November.

TOURMALINE

Tourmaline is a fascinating stone that comes in a range of colors including dark emerald green, pink, red, clear, blue, red violet and black. There is even a "watermelon tourmaline" with pink turning abruptly to green in one crystal. In fact, this abrupt change of color is one of the distinctive characteristics of tourmaline.

Tourmaline is so strongly dichroic that as you turn it from axis to axis two distinct shades can be seen. If you look at tourmaline through one lens of a pair of Polaroid sunglasses and turn the lens or the stone, it will seem to go from dark to light. This test will help you identify true tourmaline from any imitations. Also, like topaz and amber, tourmaline develops a strong electrical charge when it is rubbed, and will pick up bits of tissue paper.

Very good specimens of tourmaline are mined in Maine, as well as Russia, Brazil and South Africa. Its hardness is 7–7½, a high enough reading to ensure good polish—but the tourmaline crystals in the raw are often so beautiful that they are set as is to form bold, arresting modern jewelry.

TURQUOISE

The "sky stone" of the American Indians and the ancient talisman of the Turks (from whom it gets its name), turquoise is a much loved stone deeply tied to history and magic, and full of folklore.

It is a rather soft stone (Mohs scale: 6), an opaque blue or bluish green, sometimes with veins or pieces of the matrix ore in it. Particularly admired by the Indians, this veined turquoise is often featured in the fine silver jewelry that comes from the Southwest.

Turquoise has a smooth waxy finish which is actually porous, and will absorb dirt (or dirty dishwater, if you wash with your rings on) and will darken or turn green. Once the color changes, it can't really be restored, though there are plenty of tales afloat about how to bury stones in the earth or soak them in chemicals to get back (or synthesize) the most desired color, clear sky blue. Greenish turquoise is often stained to improve the color, but usually these stains fade or wash out. Turquoise is sometimes impregnated with color, or with a kind of plastic which bonds the color into the stone, giving it a glassy, fake finish. These stones are to be avoided! Very often the process starts, not even with a stone, but with turquoise dust, which (like *ambroid*, in the case of amber) is fused into something that looks like turquoise, but is of far less value and beauty. Much of the cheap "Indian" jewelry sold on the streets and in novelty stores is made of this kind of "turquoise" or perhaps even of glass or plastic, and the "silver" is often base metal (also called "white metal"). True Indian-crafted turquoise jewelry usually contains stones with matrix, and should be hand-crafted of sterling silver (marked), or coin silver (sometimes marked "coin").

Turquoise has been highly esteemed in the Eastern countries for centuries, and turquoise beads and pendants were worn by the ancient Chinese as well as by the even more ancient Egyptians. Horses were hung with turquoise talismans as a way of protecting them and their riders, and the stone was also believed to protect a maiden's virtue. In the sixteenth century, only men were allowed to wear turquoise, and it was believed to have special powers—but only if it had been given as a gift.

Turquoise is noncrystalline, and usually occurs in nodules or veins in sandstone. The stones the ancient Egyptians wore and loved probably came from mines along the coast of the Sinai Peninsula. At one time these mines were lost, but now they have been found again, and are still the sources for some stones. You can distinguish turquoise from these mines by the curved blue and dark blue "stripes," similar to the ones on malachite. The American Southwest produces fine turquoise too, in Arizona, New Mexico, Nevada and California, though this stone is not as dark as the Middle Eastern variety. The very best turquoise in the world comes from one mine in Iran on a mountaintop called Ali-Mersad. This turquoise, of the purest, brightest robin's egg blue, is rare and costly. Most of it finds its way to India or the Soviet.

If the pieces used are very small, it can be very hard to tell real turquoise from synthetic. In large nuggets, the problems are obvious: has the stone been treated, impregnated, reconstituted, and so on. But in small particles, glass, plastic and other stones are really very difficult to detect. If you look at your stones through a 10-power loupe and see bubbles, you are probably looking at glass. If the color wipes off with a bit of ammonia, clearly the turquoise has been stained (and not very expertly). Artificially bonded materials will turn a drop of hydrochloric acid greenish yellow, which real turquoise won't do. And most of the other stones used are heavier and harder than the real thing.

Turquoise is the birthstone for December.

WATER OPAL (see OPAL)

ZIRCON

Zircon is probably the most misunderstood and under-rated of all the semiprecious stones. True zircons are fiery, fascinating gems. Though their hardness is only 6½–7½, they rival diamonds in luster and splashy display of color—and that has, in a way, been their downfall. Because they have so often been mistaken for diamonds and substituted for them, zircons, beauties in their own right, have come to be regarded as second rate, diamond stand-ins.

Zircons occur naturally in several colors—yellow, green, blue and various shades of brown. Most common are the reddish browns. When treated with heat, most of the red-dish brown stones respond by changing to a clear, colorless and sparkling shade.

Zircons are strongly doubly refractive, a trait that dis-tinguishes them from synthetic spinels as well as genuine diamonds. Glass, also sometimes mistaken for zircon, has nothing like its fire, and is, of course, singly refractive, as well as much softer and warmer to the touch. Zircons are usually cut in their own variation of the brilliant cut, called the *zircon cut*, with a few extra facets around the culet.

Yellowish red zircons are called *hyacinth* or *jacinth*, and are truly beautiful gemstones. Straw yellow zircons from Ceylon are called *jargoons*, and sometimes that term is also used to describe the heat-treated colorless stones. Most zircons are mined in Indochina and then sent to be cut and marketed at Bangkok, but they also come from Norway, France, Australia and Burma.

Pearls

No upheavals of the earth created pearls; no explosions are needed to blow them from the mines; no faceters and cutters cleave and shine them. Deep in the dark ocean a living creature builds them, slowly, layer by iridescent layer, and when they are found—whether by chance or by design—they are already perfect, unchangeable.

The pearl's history goes back to the beginning of recorded time. For sea cultures, river people, American Indians and Egyptians, pearls were part of the treasure stored up for a future life.

Like jade, pearls have a powerful mystique that defies the buy-and-sell values surrounding other gems. This is not to say that fine pearls are not expensive. They are. And of course there are people who deal in them, trade them and invest in them. But most pearls, even the finest, are bought to be worn. They grow more beautiful with wear; they are enhanced by contact with human skin. In contrast to other gems, few pearls are bought solely for investment, and few spend their time in vaults. Pearls are *loved*.

There are many old legends about what pearls are and how they were developed. One claims that they were drops

of rain that fell into the oyster and were magically transformed. Hindu folklore says that pearls were drawn from
the sea by the great god Vishnu as a wedding present for
his daughter. They are still favorite wedding presents—a
proof of the staying power of a legend. In a Brahman
prayer, these words appear: "The bone of the gods turned
into pearl." And we all know Shakespeare's beautiful chant:
"Full fathom five thy father lies, of his bones are coral
made; These are the pearls that were his eyes; Nothing of
him that doth fade, But doth suffer a sea-change, into
something rich and strange."

Rich and strange—a good description of pearls. In a
famous story Cleopatra invited her future lover, Mark An-
tony, to the costliest dinner in history. She dissolved one
of a pair of fabulous pearls in a glass of wine, then drank
it! This illustrates another principle of gem—and pearl—
lore: if one is good, two are better. One fine gem has a
price; two matched ones are much more than twice the
value. So Cleopatra's gesture really had class *and* subtlety!

In fact, the history of pearls goes back at least thirty-
five hundred years before Christ was born, when these sea
treasures were worshiped as moon symbols, rain symbols,
fertility gems, harbingers of good fishing and safety on
the waters. Seacoast people traded and treasured them,
along with shells and mother-of-pearl, believing them to
be magical and valuable. Some peoples believed the pearl
was guarded by dragons and serpents in the depths of the
ocean, and that it was the eye of a fabulous creature. We
know that the Dravidians of Southern India traded pearls
and shells with Sumerians and Egyptians thirty centuries
before Christ. The ancient city of Korkai was the pearl
capital and the center of a religious cult that worshiped
pearls and shells.

The treasures of the pharaohs were studded with pearls,
and the Queen of Sheba is said to have brought a great
pearl as a present when she visited King Solomon. The

114

kohl dust used as eye makeup by the Egyptians and others was in fact made of pulverized pearl, and had symbolic as well as cosmetic meaning. One of the oldest and finest pieces of pearl jewelry ever found is a necklace of an ancient Persian princess that dates back to the fourth century B.C. The real wonder is that the pearls have lasted through the centuries, because unlike gold or gemstones, pearls are attacked by acids and other chemicals in the soil and air, and deteriorate if they are not protected. The Greeks and Romans used pearls as love tokens; Julius Caesar gave a giant pearl to his mistress Servilia and both Caligula and Nero were said to wear a coronet of pearls around their brows.

In those days the lower classes were not allowed to wear pearls—an odd rule in light of the fact that, unlike most gems, pearls were to be found by both rich and poor and needed no skill or workmanship by men to bring out their special beauty. Fishermen found them, children playing in the water found them, women washing or hunting for food found them, and throughout history they were usually worn and loved by rich and poor alike. Of course the best ones made their way into the hands of kings and emperors—a valuable pearl found by a humble fisherman was quickly traded for favors or food. But more modest pearls were kept and treasured—as symbols of fertility, chastity, purity, love, good fortune or even as an aphrodisiac—more widely than any other costly gem.

Pearls do appear in the Bible: "Neither cast ye your pearls before swine," and the Book of Revelation's description of heaven's "twelve gates were twelve pearls." In fact, church robes and vestments were embroidered with pearls as the Christian Church gained in wealth and power.

In both North and South America, pearls were known since earliest times. Indian burial mounds in Ohio have yielded the remains of pearl jewelry, and John Smith, the English explorer who married Pocahontas, described her father Powhatan's treasure house as being full of pearls—in this case, freshwater pearls that came from mussels living in the pure water of the rivers. The Indians bored them with hot wires or drills and wore them for ceremonial occasions and adornment. Early drawings of Indians show women and children wearing ropes of pearls around their necks, twined in their hair or on the robes of the chiefs. One tribe even made artificial pearls—baked clay beads covered with many thin layers of mica. When on his second voyage Columbus saw pearls on the island he christened Margarita and failed to mention this to King Ferdinand, he was thrown into jail in chains until he could convince the greedy monarch that the oversight was unintentional. South America proved to be rich in ocean pearls that were far finer than the freshwater pearls of the north. The remains of great pearls have been found in the ruins of the Yucatan and Peru, which led archeologists to believe that they were used in religious ceremonies and for tribute, much as they had been in ancient India. Montezuma, the great Aztec chieftain, gave the explorer Cortez great quantities of pearls in an effort to appease the Spaniards' passion for treasure, but in fact they just whetted Cortez's appetite, and pearls, like gold, became a factor in the brutal conquest and enslavement of the New World.

One pearl discovered in this period, La Peregrina, has a fascinating history that illustrates how pearls have been prized and coveted throughout the ages. This pearl was discovered in the Gulf of Panama around 1560, a time when Spanish slaves were chained and forced to dive for unbearably long days, and fed only the flesh of the creatures they brought up from the waters. The slave who found La Peregrina was given his freedom as a reward, and his lucky master, who sent it home to Philip II of Spain, got a title and lands for his trouble. The giant pearl weighed about 50 carats, a pear-shaped beauty too perfect even to be drilled. When Philip married Mary Tudor, Henry VIII's sickly and homely daughter that year, he gave her La Peregrina. When she died, religious Mary left Philip the pearl, and he had it set in the crown of the Blessed Virgin at Guadalupe, but later it surfaced again among the royal jewels of Spain. In 1605 Queen Margarita wore it; in 1700 it was briefly part of a pair of earrings (in tandem with another great pear-shaped pearl from America); later that century it was mentioned by a courtier as gracing the king's hat. The pearl was so famous that it was recognized whenever it was worn. In 1813 when Joseph Bonaparte left the Spanish throne, he took La Peregrina along and gave it to his stepniece Hortense, who passed it on to Louis Napoleon. Louis, bankrupt, took it to England, asked his friend the Marquis of Abercorn to help him dispose of it, and ended up selling it to the marquis himself, who fell in love with it. But the marquis' wife found the huge pearl a problem. Since it had never been bored and was so heavy, she kept losing it—once in the train of a lady going into a state supper ahead of her, once in the Windsor Castle sofa cushions—until she finally rebelled and had it drilled, though it impaired the value, so she could wear it as much as she liked in safety. When last noted, the pearl was still owned by the Abercorn family.

My colored-gems dealer friend tells me of another giant pearl—perhaps the same one—which had never been out of the possession of a great English family until it came on the market, privately and secretly, and passed through his hands. This glorious gem was pictured in a famous painting, a pearl of great value and fascinating history. He sold it to a famous movie actress, and when he visited her later to sell her an emerald, he found that the pearl had been chewed up by her poodle!

Very few people know about the humble beginnings of the great pearl boom in America. It all started in Notch Brook, New Jersey, when a Paterson shoemaker who liked to eat mussels for dinner chewed on something hard. That something was a giant pearl, nearly 400 grains (100 carats). Had it not been cooked, the pearl would have been worth $25,000. A few days later a fine but smaller pink pearl (raw!) was found by a local carpenter and sold to Charles Tiffany in New York for $1,500. And the rush was on. In 1857 over $100,000 worth of pearls were stripped out of the Notch Brook area, and the Paterson bonanza was over. But throughout the country, boys waded through streams finding mussels with their toes; families went on pearl-finding picnics financed by pearl entrepreneurs who would give them all they could eat plus a day in the country for all the pearls they could find; and huge mother-of-pearl factories were springing up on the banks of rivers to make buttons and buckles and costume jewelry from the mountains of leftover shells.

These American freshwater pearls came in many colors: soft gray and pink, cream and white, metallic green, purplish brown, dark blue and silver. They came from Ohio, Wisconsin, Pennsylvania, Texas, New Jersey, Arkansas, Tennessee, Maine, Massachusetts, Connecticut, Georgia, Florida, New York—nearly every state in the Union.

The rich Eastern society women scorned freshwater pearls and preferred the European "orientals," but American women wore them incessantly. Many of the freshwaters were *baroques*, of irregular shape, while most sea pearls were round. The old standards for consummate natural sea pearls were perfect roundness (rarely attained but often closely approximated), perfect color (and the preferred color was a creamy white with a blush of soft pink, or *rosé*) and fine iridescent luster, called "orient." The best pearls were large and heavy, either perfectly matched in a strand, or (less valued but still important) graduated two by two with the largest pearl centered in the front. These classic standards still apply.

For baroques or freshwater pearls, however, odd shapes and unusual colors—if they are aesthetically pleasing—

are desirable, and though many people look for large size in baroques as well, tiny seed pearls have always been popular, particularly in delicate lacy patterns or massed in huge collars and chokers—to justify the tedious (and costly) work of stringing them. Of course dyeing or tinting is not desirable in either sea or freshwater pearls, and poorly placed drill holes that make the pearls hang unevenly as well as roughness or thin *nacre* (the material the pearl is made of) are considered to be major flaws in any pearl. In short, the free-for-all feeling that characterizes freshwater pearls—and that was an intrinsic part of the nineteenth-century American personality—made freshwaters probably the most popular jewelry worn at the time. Bibs, chokers, dog collars, ropes, rings, brooches, buttons, studs and all manner of adornments boasted beautiful pearls of all sizes and colors fished from our own waters. Even engagement rings were centered with a pearl. Jewelry stores featured local pearls; fortunes were built on pearls. Even women with modest incomes owned a few pearls.

And then the pearls ran out. The overfishing, combined with the beginnings of industrial pollution contributed to the disappearance of pearl-bearing mussels from American streams and rivers. By the end of World War I the American pearl bonanza was over, though the shell industry remained, and it's hard to foresee a time when our waterways will again be peaceful enough to grow beautiful pearls.

Fine freshwater pearls have been found in other countries, and can occur in any mussels. The best quality freshwaters are from a type of mussel known as *Unio*, which is found in the rivers of Scotland, North Wales, Ireland, Germany and Austria. Unfortunately, these countries too are now highly industrialized, and the production of pearls today is very limited. But in the nineteenth century the gray Scottish pearls were a favorite of canny Queen Victoria, who did the same thing for British pearls that she did for Australia's opals. By wearing and advertising the beauty of the Scottish pearls, she made them popular.

Freshwater pearls are still produced in small quantities, and there is always a good chance that in the few remaining wild and untrammeled corners of the world there are pearl mussels growing more beautiful gems that we'll discover some day and not pillage and pollute out of existence. However, in Lake Biwa in Japan, marvelously lustrous white, purple, blue, bronze and pink baroques and ovals and rounds are still being fished, but rumor is that this lake, too, is falling prey to industrial pollution and the great, lustrous Biwa pearls (my own favorites among the freshwaters) will soon be unobtainable.

Though the ancients had so many fanciful ideas about the origin of pearls, we now know that all pearls develop in much the same way. A bit of foreign matter is lodged between the shell of the mollusk and its soft body, which is surrounded by soft tissue called a *mantle*. This mantle secretes a material that actually forms the three parts of the shell: the dark outer layer made up of *conchiolin*, an inner layer of iridescent mother-of-pearl, and a layer of shelly calcium carbonate sandwiched between them. When any irritating substance, like a grain of sand, gets into the shell, the mantle secretes *nacre*, the same material that makes up the inner mother-of-pearl layer. Most often the nacre eases the problem by covering the particle and cementing it to the inner shell. When found, this lump of nacre would be a *blister pearl*, flat on one side, roundish on the other. These blister pearls, or *mobes*, are often used in jewelry. A favorite way is to attach them to earring backs as pearl-button earrings.

When the intruder in the shell is a tiny living creature, like a parasite, which can move around and thus cannot be cemented to the shell, the mollusk traps the offending bit of matter in a sort of sac, and secretes around it. The parasite dies, but the mantle keeps secreting, perhaps for many years, and a round or roundish pearl, often of great size, results. These round pearls are known as *cyst* or *mantle pearls*.

Sea pearls as well as freshwaters come in a variety of colors, but it is the white or creamy rosés that bring the highest price. Staining is really not very successful, because the natural iridescence cannot really be matched, but some dark pearls are treated by soaking them in silver nitrate (the chemical used on film) and then exposing them to sunlight or ultraviolet rays. Thus "developed" and buffed to brightness, they look like beautiful natural black pearls, and are hard to detect.

Experts say that the finest pearls in the world come from the banks of the Persian Gulf, where the *Pinctada vulgaris* oyster has been producing creamy white pearls for more than two thousand years. In fact, the reason natural sea pearls are known as "oriental" is that they were first discovered in the Orient—in the Persian Gulf, in the Gulf of Mannar, off the coast of Bombay, along the Red Sea. Natural pearls are still fished from these waters, but in diminishing amounts, and then shipped to Bombay to be drilled. Fine pearls also come from the South Pacific, from the northern coast of Australia and from the waters off Central and South America. The Persian Gulf pearls are still brought up by bare-skinned divers, who jump unprotected from sailing vessels into thirty to ninety feet of water to haul the pearl-bearing oysters up in string bags. The Australian pearls, large and white or golden yellow, are fished by divers in protective suits. White and bronze pearls are still taken from the waters around Venezuela, near the Margarita (which means "pearl") Islands where Columbus first saw pearls in the New World; these are bronze or white. Many of the Mexican pearls, taken from the Gulf of California, are black and deep gray, and gray or yellow pearls come from the Gulf of Panama. But very, very few natural pearls are brought to the Bombay drillers now.

What brought an end to the centuries-long productivity of these great pearl fisheries?

First of all, the Depression leveled the great fortunes of this country and people started selling instead of buying gems and pearls. Then, just as we were climbing out of that disaster, World War II came along and the country's collective consciousness shifted far away from frivolity and luxury. But the sharpest blow to natural pearls came from the new industry of cultured pearls, which sprang up in Japan and gradually weaned the whole world away from natural, often uneven and hard to match "accidental" pearls to an acceptance of uniform, predictable, man-induced ones.

As far as we know, the very first cultured pearls came from the Red Sea around the second century A.D., when the Arabs pricked oysters to stimulate them into producing nacre. Later, Jesuit missionaries in China described experiments in which they would insert seed pearls or clay beads into mussels, and then feed the hosts with a ginseng and honey mixture to promote the growing of pearls. In those times pearls were used in medicines as well as for adornment, and were prized for magic properties they supposedly granted not only to their wearers, but to their ingesters. By the thirteenth century the German priest Albertus Magnus claimed they were good for "mental diseases, affections of the heart...hemorrhage and dysentery." England's Sir Francis Bacon believed that *aqua perlata*, a concoction made from pearls dissolved in an acid like lemon juice and then imbibed, would cure a variety of ills, including melancholia, tearing of the eyes, weak nerves— and that it could, in fact, even revive the dead.

By the late Middle Ages, the theory that an irritant in the shell of a mollusk is what caused it to create a pearl prevailed over some of the more fanciful and magical ideas about the origins and powers of pearls. In seventeenth-century China, little Buddha figures were inserted into live mussels and the ensuing mother-of-pearl idols were widely prized. Around the middle of the eighteenth century the Swedish scientist Linnaeus claimed that he could produce tiny seed pearls in any pearl-bearing shell by poking a wire into a living mussel and inserting a bit of limestone. His technique of *culturing* spread around the world.

Finally, in 1896, a Japanese noodle peddler named Kokichi Mikimoto succeeded in producing the first commercially successful cultured pearls. He synthesized the work done all over the world into one technique of inserting seed pearls ground with salt into oyster shells to produce round, beautiful, "real" pearls. Mikimoto was a man possessed. He lived his life for these cultured pearls; his mission was to grow them, improve them and to prove to the world that they were the genuine article.

He was so successful in this effort that cultured pearls, which, when first marketed, were considered inferior to natural pearls, now command a lion's share of the market. In the twenties, a cultured pearl necklace was not something a person of great wealth would buy. It was a modest gift, low in price, pretty and polite, but not elegant or luxurious. Today cultured pearls are worn by society's trendsetters and they can cost hundreds of thousands of dollars. They rival oriental pearls in beauty—in fact, it truly takes X-ray testing to tell the difference between the finest oriental and the finest cultured pearl—and only the finest oriental could rival the cultured pearl in roundness and uniformity of color and size. Some experts say that the luster of oriental pearls is finer than that of the cultured ones, but no expert can absolutely guarantee to distinguish one from the other without an internal examination. Consequently, the price of real, natural oriental pearls has plummeted. A natural pearl necklace is still more costly than one made of cultured pearls, but the margin has decreased dramatically. In contrast to the other precious gems—which have not really been hurt at all by man-made substitutes—the market for natural pearls has been depressed by man-induced ones. Why? To a great extent it is a function of Mikimoto's genius: his passion for cultured pearls, coupled with his business acumen helped him convince the whole world that all the magic, mystery, beauty and power invested in pearls throughout the centuries could apply to "real, cultured" pearls—which were more plentiful, more predictable, better priced and better marketed.

The value of cultured pearls, too, has soared. Mikimoto died in 1955, but the empire he founded, like the De Beers Corporation, still controls the production, sale and price of cultured pearls around the world.

If I had $75,000 to $100,000 to invest in fine jewelry, I would track down and buy the best, biggest, heaviest, best-colored, best-matched (exact matches, not graduated), longest strand of real natural orientals I could find, and put them safely away. (Remember, the key word here is "invest.")

I would visit them occasionally to keep them happy, expose them to sunlight and fresh air, wear them (who would believe they were real?) to help them retain their luster, wipe them off afterward with silk or chamois, protect them from acid substances (perfume, or hairspray, or—even more insidious—acid from a plastic box or jewelry case), and have them restrung periodically so that no dirt on the string could penetrate the pearls. And then eventually I would put them up for sale, at a time in the world when real natural orientals were even scarcer and more exotic than they are now and cultured pearls were even more widespread and plentiful. I'm sure they would bring a fortune.

How can you tell cultured from natural pearls? Only a handful of experts will confidently claim they can tell anything by eye alone, or even by louping. Some are guided by the evenness of cultured pearls, but that is certainly not a sure test. Some say cultureds have a slight greenish tinge, while naturals have a better rosé. But, as we've seen, natural pearls can be nearly every color in the rainbow, so color alone is not a reliable measure of a pearl's value. A dealer may claim that touching his teeth to pearls is a foolproof test, and while this technique does measure the slight gritty texture of all real pearls, it's hardly a reliable method for distinguishing natural pearls from cultureds.

In the twenties, when cultured pearls first flooded the market, many systems were developed to distinguish this new kind of pearl from the old variety. Fluorescence, specific gravity and density tests were used, but none gave conclusive results. The key to the problem is that natural pearls have a slightly different internal construction. They begin with a parasite, which eventually disappears, or a tiny grain of sand; cultured pearls are centered around a larger bit of shell or other matter.

The *endoscope*, a needlelike instrument which shines a powerful beam of light through the pearl from the inside out, or the *pearl microscope*, which uses a similar kind of probe to reflect the material on the inside of the drill hole, can help detect how the pearl was formed, and therefore if it was cultured. *X-ray* is also a reliable method that can be used even when the pearl is undrilled. But most jewelers are not equipped with these sophisticated tools, and none of them—no matter what they say—has X-ray vision. Therefore, if you really want to know if the pearls you buy are oriental pearls or man-induced, cultured ones (and you should), get a GIA or similar certificate before you buy or as a condition of the sale.

Frankly, fake pearls are usually easy to detect, even by a novice. For the most part they are made of glass, covered, well or badly, with some kind of ground mother-of-pearl (sometimes powdered fish scales). At the drill hole you can usually see—with the naked eye or a loupe—the place where the pearl covering stops and the inside material is bare. If you run the tip of your teeth over the surface, or look at it closely with your loupe, you will not see or feel the graininess that is characteristic of the nacre when it is secreted by a live mollusk. The pressure of the point of a pin against a fake pearl will produce a slight dent in the painted-on surface, but in a real pearl this pressure will not blemish the nacre.

Biwa pearls, the beautiful cultureds from Lake Biwa, Japan, and a small number of other cultured pearls, particularly the ones from Australia, are produced by inserting a piece of mussel tissue, which eventually disappears, leaving behind nothing to indicate that the pearl was cultured except the particular sheen, color and shape that these pearls usually have, plus the manner in which the nacre was laid down, all of which can be seen by use of the sophisticated instruments already mentioned. Cultured pearls made this way are called *nonnucleated*.

When pearls are first gathered, they are sorted by size and shape and graded by color. Round "necklace" pearls are drilled through the center, and mobes or blister pearls, which are flat on one side, are drilled partway through and cemented to a metal peg for earrings or studs. "Chinese drilling," or off-center drilling near the top or bottom, is not as desirable, and crooked drill holes detract from the value of the pearl.

The price of a pearl depends on its size, color, origin, shape and weight, and unless the pearl is very unusual, it is usually evaluated in groups or bunches. Pearls are weighed in *grains* (four grains to the carat; one carat is $\frac{1}{5}$ of a gram) or, in Japan, *mommes*. (Each momme is 75 grains, or 18¾ carats.)

Caring for pearls is simple and essential. Most important, never let them come in contact with acid; it will spoil them. This means no spraying of perfume or hairspray while you're wearing them, and if you have pearl rings, a certain amount of care in hand washing and in preparing food is necessary. Air is good for pearls, and they should not be put away in sealed plastic bags or left in closed boxes in the dark for long periods of time. In fact, pearls actually do improve with wear, and some people are "pearl healers" whose skin chemistry is beneficial to the apearance of the pearl, while others have such acidity in their systems that they harm the luster of pearls by wearing them and should probably only wear them over clothing.

There is an old saying that pearls should be restored once a year by washing them in sea water, but I don't agree. In fact, I would suspect that salt water would rot the silk string holding them. I do know that a rinse with fresh clear water will certainly not hurt them, and some of my pearl-loving friends use mild soap, often the facial kind, to give their pearls an occasional bath. A gentle wiping with a soft cloth (silk is best) or a chamois is good after wearing, too.

The most important step in maintaining the beauty of your pearls is to have them restrung frequently: about once a year if you wear them often, whenever the cord stretches, or if you see that the pearls have play between the knots. The danger is not only that the string might break; a broken string really only endangers the life of one pearl (by the way, all pearls must be strung with knots in between). The most formidable threat to the safety of your pearls is the dirt and perspiration that get on the string and then works its way into the inside of the pearl—which, whether natural or cultured, is really its weakest part. This dirt will corrode and darken the color of your pearls.

Firm knotting keeps each pearl in its place and the knots themselves close up the vulnerable drill holes. So, remember—restringing is important.

Because restringing is difficult and expensive, many people avoid it, or try to learn how to do it themselves. You can learn to restring, but it is a painstaking and lengthy procedure. If you are agile with your hands, though, here's how to do it.

First, buy a *threading needle* and strong *silk thread* in a neutral color from a hobby or bead store. It is also worthwhile to buy a *bead board*, if you can find one. This wooden board has grooves to hold beads, and with it you can lay a whole string of pearls out in order—essential if you are working with graduated pearls. The threading needle is long and very thin with a relatively long eye and will go into a much narrower drill hole or bore than a regular sewing needle. You will also need some white (colorless) mild glue, such as jeweler's glue. Be sure to set aside plenty of time so you can do the whole operation in one sitting.

First, carefully count the beads. Then cut the string between each bead and, one at a time, lay the beads out on the board in the same order as they were in the necklace. Cut the clasp off, too, and clean off any bits of string or glue that may adhere to it. Now thread your needle, doubling the thread first so that you actually have a four-ply length of silk. The whole strand should be at least two and a half times as long as the necklace. Carefully knot one half of the clasp to the end of your thread, and glue the knot. When the glue has dried (and only the tiniest bit applied with a toothpick is necessary), pick up the first (smallest, if graduated) pearl on your needle and slip it down over the thread to the clasp. Now make an open knot by passing the thread around in a circle and putting the needle through it. Then, keeping the circle from closing into a knot, put the point of the needle inside it and slowly and carefully move it until it rests right up against the pearl. Throughout this process one hand is on the needle, the other is carefully pulling the thread. At the very last and trickiest part, keep the closing knot against the pearl as you slowly pull it tight, "steering" it with the needle. If there is space between the knot and the pearl, let go of the tension on the thread and pull the knot open again with the needle. When you get it just right and the closing knot is right up against the pearl, slowly draw it tight and, at the last, withdraw the point of the needle. Now you can breathe a sigh of relief. You have made one knot.

This process is repeated, pearl by pearl, until the whole strand is strung. At the other end, do the same thing with the clasp as you would with a pearl, finally drawing the knot tight, and again, sealing it against slippage by touching it lightly with glue. It is very important that the glue never touch the pearls, and that the glued knot stays flexible so that it doesn't rub against a neighboring pearl.

Some expert threaders leave an equal length of thread at the beginning and end of the strand. After completing the procedure they rethread the needle with these ends and pass them up through a few pearls, then cut off what's left of the thread. This makes a neater, safer closure. There are other similar tricks that will make pearl stringing a bit easier, but, if you are going to do it properly, it will always be a long, tedious job. That is why jewelers charge so much to do it and why most of them won't actually undertake it themselves but send it out to an expert. If you do allow your jeweler to send your pearls out to be restrung, make sure that you count them first and have him write the number and size of the pearls on your receipt. Be sure, too, that you are dealing with a merchant you can trust; it would be very easy for him to switch pearls on an unsuspecting buyer.

At some time you might also want to add to your pearls or to have the style of stringing changed. Both of these procedures are quite simple. Make sure, though, that any new pearls are matched to the old ones for color, size and luster. It used to be a "grandma" tradition to give children a pearl a year, a small gift that grows into a big one. In fact, such a necklace costs far, far more and is not as well matched or graduated as when all the pearls have been purchased at once.

Things to look out for when buying pearls are poor or

crooked drilling (the pearls will hang awkwardly on the string), poorly matched size and color, bubbles or bumps on the surface, uneven shapes (unless you are buying baroques), thin or even nonexistent nacre (bare spots), lackluster pearls without iridescence or life and stained, dyed or overbleached pearls (cultured pearls are customarily bleached to improve their color, but if they are overbleached they lose their glow). When purchasing your pearl necklace, it is a good idea to place a few necklaces side by side and compare them. As with other gems, light and reflected color are important features to consider. Most pearls are "dressed up" by showing them on black velvet. You would do better to look at them on a white handkerchief, and more important, to hold them up against your skin. One shade may be much more flattering than another to your particular complexion. Large, ungraduated choker-length pearls will not flatter a short, thick neck, and a long strand of tiny beads will look awful on someone who's tall and thin. Above all, the pearls should highlight your most attractive features.

In case you should need any further reason to buy pearls, they are the birthstones for June.

Antique Jewelry

It is certainly a wonderful experience to buy and own a new piece of jewelry, and there is also a special excitement in having jewelry designed especially for you. But if you love the past and value painstaking hand work, your best bet may be to buy a fine piece of antique jewelry. Some of the most beautiful and unusual gems are found in antique jewelry: rare and fine Kashmir sapphires; demantoid garnets from the Urals that are not even on the market anymore; early Colombian emeralds of startling color and clarity and Russian emeralds from mines that almost disappeared at the death of the czar. Workmanship from the days when time was no object and machines couldn't fool the eye the way they can today, timeless styles that have been treasured and passed on for generations, history and provenance and fascinating pedigrees—these are the intangibles of antique jewelry. And the tangibles? Modern jewelry is primarily appraised in terms of the major stones; while setting and style do play a role, it is only a minimal one. And because new jewelry is "keystoned," or marked up as much as 100 percent, should you want to sell a piece after you've worn it for a while, its value would have decreased drastically unless, in the interim, the price of the stones had at least doubled.

131

In fact, though some jewelers make it a condition of sale that they'll take back jewelry for the same price within a certain guaranteed time period, in most cases the moment you buy the piece its resale value goes down; like a car, the instant your jewel is bought, it is considered "used."

In the case of antique jewelry, however, the situation is different. There are still markups, and the retail price you pay is not the same as the dealer's or wholesale price you would be offered should you want to sell, but there are important distinctions. First of all, the setting, workmanship, style, rarity and age of a piece all determine its price, and these factors don't change or diminish as you hold on to it. In fact, since part of its value is derived from its age, the passing of time only enhances its value. Of course there is still the matter of retail versus wholesale price, but even so, all other things being equal in these inflationary times, antique jewelry, which passes certain tests of excellence, when held for a few years nearly always survives the fluctuations of our economy, and often rises in value. Therefore, antique jewelry is considered by most people to be a sound investment.

However, investment (even the soundest one) is never the first reason why anyone should buy any kind of jewelry. Jewelry's aesthetic value is what lie at the core of its ability to give its owner pleasure. And antique jewelry offers quite a lot on that score.

At any antique show and in many shops, there is a bewildering display of jewelry in all price ranges, periods and styles that is labeled—or mislabeled—"antique." How do you know the good from the bad, the real from the fake, the worth-buying from the practically worthless?

Antique jewelry, like antique clothing, can be distinguished by *periods*, and in order to buy it knowledgeably you should be able to recognize the characteristics of each period.

Ancient jewelry is loosely taken to mean any adornment

that can be traced back to ancient times, specifically the Greek, Roman, Scythian, Egyptian, pre-Columbian periods. Jewelry from these lost cultures is probably not too wearable today. The exception to this is jade, which can easily be hung on a silk cord and enjoyed today as it was centuries ago. But since alloying was not understood in ancient times, the gold is always of a very high karat and is therefore too soft for daily wear. Silver from long ago is usually badly discolored or tarnished if it is very old or has been buried or exposed to the elements, and is also fragile. Very old earrings were probably permanently attached to very old ears, and without extensive alteration would not be suitable for wearing today. One of the cardinal rules of antique jewelry is: don't change or repair or restyle or replace *anything* unless it is absolutely necessary. Repairs diminish value, and if you love old things you want to shepherd them through time without harming or modernizing them; it is important to send them into the next generation exactly as they were when they first came into your possession. Ancient bronze jewelry is very heavy and hard to wear, and may discolor if exposed to the pollution and the modern substances you handle every day. So in general, very old jewelry is not wearable, and should be purchased only if you fall in love with it and understand that your pleasure in it probably will be confined to owning and looking rather than really wearing it.

Jewelry from the Middle Ages onward is much more wearable, and, though it is hard to find, often in poor condition, and very expensive, it is still interesting and pleasurable to own. The extremely rare posy rings of the sixteenth century, made of plain gold or silver with quaint love poems inscribed on them, religious jewelry, very old pendants, beads and gold chains can still be worn today and enjoyed. You can see jewelry like this in museum collections; it would only be in very special antique shops or private sales that you would ever have a chance to buy such treasures yourself. There is one sixteenth-century ring that I saw in an English dealer's catalog that I still regret not buying. It was a simple gold circlet with a small stone but on the inside these words were inscribed: "Grante me mercie, for Godde's sake praye for me; with this gifte I yield myself to you." Although it's probably far too frail to wear on a finger, I'd love to hang it around my neck, or perhaps even just have it to look at.

The years 1714 to 1830 during the reign of four English Georges is known as the Georgian period. By this time jewelry had ceased to be the exclusive possession of the upper classes; gradually more and more of it came into existence, and as a result there is much of it still around to be seen and bought. It is still comparatively rare, however, and the passion for things Georgian keeps the price high. Georgian gold is high-karat (18 or better) and therefore easily dented, but is not as fragile as ancient, unalloyed gold, which is so soft you can literally bend it with your fingers. Styles were light and airy in the eighteenth century, as was gold jewelry, so Georgian rings and chains may have a substantial look, but the gold is usually light in weight, in thin sheets rather than thick, heavy, solid chunks, as it would be a century later. The stones in rings were often *foiled*—that is, backed with colored metal to give a more desirable color. Diamonds, especially, were foiled, as were *pastes*—glass gems cut and polished as carefully as real ones and set in silver to give them a "whiter" look, so most Georgian rings have closed settings. Rings that are foiled should not get wet, so Georgian rings, though they are beautiful, should be taken off whenever you wash, and hence are rather a bother. How then did Georgian rings last? Did the Georgians keep taking them off and putting them on? Actually, soap and water weren't all that popular in the eighteenth century, and aristocrats who wore fine jewelry certainly weren't doing their own dishes;

so that's why foiled rings have survived to be worn in the twentieth century.

Thanks to Peruzzi's discovery of the brilliant cut in 1700, the popularity of diamonds soared, and the eighteenth century came to be known as the Age of Diamonds. Memorial jewelry, enameled or crafted with hair or ivory, was popular at this time, too; used to commemorate the death of a loved one, memorial rings were customarily given out to all the guests at funerals. Usually they bore a name and death date (sometimes also a birth date) and an appropriate sentiment such as *Memento mori.*

With the exception of the very few gemstones discovered within the last hundred years, all the precious and semi-precious stones were used in Georgian jewelry, as well as many colored pastes, pearls, coral and ivory. *Cut steel* was popular, too, used even in very fancy evening jewelry; a full *parure* (complete set) of cut steel, worn at the lavish Lafayette Ball at the end of the American Revolution, is part of the collection of the Museum of the City of New York. Many of the gemstones were cut cabochon in those days, and many of the diamonds, despite the popularity of the brilliant cut, were still faceted in the old way, with a flat back and fewer faces, domed up into the beautiful *rose cut.* Real Georgian pearls were, of course, natural ori-entals—cultured pearls had not yet been marketed—but there already were fake pearls, made of wax or glass.

Georgian jewelry had quite a different look from any other style in jewelry history, and if you buy it, you should be sure to study a little bit about it, so that you are not fooled. Often antique dealers are remiss and will assure you something is at once "Georgian, English, and 14-carat." Since at that time in England all gold had to be 18-carat (remember, the American spelling is *k*arat) or better, this is impossible. If, when you point this out to the dealer he responds with "Well, that's what I was told," you will henceforth be aware of another difference between buying antique jewelry and buying new pieces: the dealer is often ignorant of the real history—and even the authenticity—of the piece. You, as the buyer, have to learn enough to evaluate what is said to you, and if you are buying a major piece, you should definitely have it appraised by someone who is an expert—not merely in jewelry, but in antique jewelry.

During her reign, which began in 1830, Queen Victoria exercised a powerful influence on fashion, jewelry, morals—you name it! There is a great deal of Victorian jewelry present today, mostly massive pieces of gold or silver reminiscent of the past. Colorful stones and showy parures were popular; sentiment was rampant. "Love" jewelry, like Mizpah pieces (see glossary) rings and brooches, hair jewelry made from the tresses of loved ones (dead or alive) and "regard" rings that spelled out the word in *r*ubies, *e*meralds, *g*arnets, *a*methysts, *r*ose quartz and *d*iamonds, were the order of the day.

Most of the jewelry from this period that is available in the United States today is English. A smaller amount is French, or from other countries in Europe. Comparatively little American jewelry was made at that time; the Puritan ethic condemning luxuries, combined with the snobbery of the rich who favored European commodities over home grown, lessened the demand for American-made ornaments. The poor and middle class might buy American—when they bought anything at all—but American-made antique jewelry is rather rare, and though it is usually simple and forthright in design, its rarity now makes it somewhat higher in price than its European counterparts. Of course, famous designers like Tiffany (who bought many of his finest pieces in Europe) made high-priced jewelry even in the nineteenth century. But in these earlier times it was mostly humble goldsmiths and a few jewelry factories that turned out machine-made pieces for the popular taste.

It is very hard to pinpoint when certain jewelry styles came into fashion, because designs overlap decades, and sometimes a piece will be so successful and so "classic" that it will reappear repeatedly through several periods. Only a very careful examination can uncover the differences between a modern and ancient Greek snake ring, for example. But at the end of the nineteenth century the Art Nouveau movement suddenly enveloped all the decorative arts, and the flowing lines, brooding women's faces, sensuous leaves, flowers and plants all marked the definitive end to the rather heavy, almost stodgy jewelry of the late Victorian period. When Victoria died in 1903, the popularity of the feminine, delicate Gibson Girl mirrored the newly graceful and slimmed-down look of jewelry. The bright colors loved by the Victorians were now muted: diamonds and moonstones were the favorite colorless stones; pearls, silver, thin gold chains, slim ring bands and high pearl dog collars were the ladylike jewelry to wear. The Art Nouveau movement made "odd" stones popular and iridescence almost a must. Opals, flawed emeralds and mother-of-pearl, as well as previously overlooked substances such as horn and shell, suddenly became popular, and craftsmen began to take pride in the uniqueness of their pieces.

After World War I, a new look surfaced—the angular, jazzy, highly colored, shiny, "modern" look of Art Deco. Even though the word "antique" is understood to mean at least one hundred years old, many antique jewelry lovers collect Art Deco for its period look, its wit and clean design and its easy wearability. Of course this has sent its prices soaring. Favored materials in Art Deco jewelry are onyx, jade, enamel, aventurine, crystal, diamonds, white gold. There is a hint of chinoiserie, too, along with its straight-line, mechanized brightness. Perhaps it's this unlikely combination that makes Art Deco jewelry so appealing and collectible.

Around the end of World War II, the Art Deco style gave way to what we call the fifties look—chunky and sensuous, all pink gold and rubies and ballerinas and kitsch. We are all nostalgic for the past, even if it's no further away than yesterday, so even this fifties material is collectible now; who knows—very soon we may be identifying and collecting the sixties, seventies and early eighties.

It is very important to understand antique jewelry if you are going to collect it. Much more than a combination of stones and metals, it represents style, history, age and philosophy. Through the years it has been a fine investment, giving great and lasting pleasure. But you must know what you are doing when you buy it.

First of all, look for pieces that are in good, preferably perfect condition. Antique dealers will cheerfully tell you that "if you were this old, you'd show your age too." While this may be true, it doesn't mean you should buy a piece merely because it is old. If it is not in really good condition—no matter what you paid for it—it has practically no resale value, and simply won't stand up to hard wear. Any symptoms of old age, like glued-in stones, very thin ring shanks, poorly mended or broken parts should be enough to turn you away from an antique piece. Especially to be avoided are gold objects that have been mended with *lead solder*; this is a pernicious and unfortunately, very common disease among antique pieces. Lead solder, which is a dull gray, almost pewterlike substance, melts at a much lower temperature than gold solder, the proper material for repairing gold. Lazy goldsmiths sometimes use it to make quick fixes—at the expense of the piece. The lead not only looks ugly, but over the years it actually eats away at the gold and will ultimately destroy it. To replace a lead-soldered repair is a hard, often impossible job; most jewelers won't even undertake it. So if you see lead solder on a gold piece (or a silver one, for that matter), don't buy it.

Very often pieces that are sold as antique jewelry really

are just that: pieces—that is, bits of a fine old necklace made into earrings, or a broken brooch center hung on a bale and passed off as a pendant. If you buy old jewelry you want it to be complete: nothing taken off, nothing added on. If you are skeptical about a particular piece, look your dealer in the eye and ask. Usually you will get the truth. But don't rely solely on his words; examine the piece yourself under a 10-power loupe. If you look at a ring under the loupe and see evidences of glue around the stone you can be pretty sure that, with a few wearings, the glue will give and the stone will fall out. Sometimes, if the prongs are loose or worn (or even broken off) and the ring is otherwise good, a jeweler can reset the stone. But as a general rule it is best to remember that all antique jewelry is a safer venture if it shows no repairs, no rebuilding, no changes at all from its original state. When buying for myself, I don't even size old rings—I just use ring guards and wear them on whatever finger they fit— but this is a personal idiosyncrasy, and most people do size rings to fit.

The major concern for most people when they buy antique jewelry—and it is a justifiable one—is that the piece will turn out to be a reproduction or a fake. More "antique jewelry" is on the market than could ever have been worn by all our grandmothers and grandfathers combined if they had covered every inch of themselves with gold and silver. Much of it is made from bits and pieces of old jewelry soldered or glued together or set onto pinbacks or earwires that bear no relationship to the originals. Even more of it is frankly (or not-so-frankly) a complete fake. How can you tell the real thing from the recent copy?

I've already cautioned you to examine each piece and look for evidence that it has been tampered with or changed in any way. By looking carefully through a loupe you should also be able to tell whether the piece has been cast or handmade. Unless it has been extremely well-finished, a cast piece shows mold marks, slight ridges where the sides of the mold were fitted together. Also, the detailing on a cast piece is not as sharp as hand-cut detailing, or even work that has been newly stamped by a machine. And remember: if a piece is cast, that doesn't necessarily mean it is new; many old pieces were cast, too. But in the bygone days of cheap hand labor and a slower work pace, the finishing on even a modest piece was usually painstaking, and mold marks were all but eliminated. In modern "repros" the work is usually hasty and careless, and with a little application, you can learn to recognize the difference.

A handmade piece will never look quite uniform under the loupe. The tool marks are visible, and if a motif is repeated, you can see the differences between the elements. In a machined piece, the perfection of the repetitions will give it away. Again, all handmade jewelry isn't old; all machined jewelry isn't reproduction. But handmade jewelry today is very high in cost; in the old days even modest pieces could be made by hand. So when a piece *is* handmade, modest in price, right for its time, well crafted and has no obvious telltale modern touches like a new safety catch (which was only marketed around World War I), or earwires that look like the ones you can buy in a hobby shop—then you are probably on safe ground, and should purchase the piece.

One of the best ways to find out whether a piece is real or not is to look the dealer firmly in the eye and say: "Is this a repro?" Usually, he will answer as truthfully as possible. Many antique dealers are not knowledgeable about old jewelry and may have been sold a bill of goods they would be pleased to get rid of by passing it on to you. Of course, if you see more than one piece of a kind on display, beware. While very few identical pieces of old jewelry survive through the centuries, there are plenty of repros cast from the same mold.

One style cluttered with repros is Art Nouveau, partly

because of its popularity (and subsequent high price, which makes reproduction a lucrative business), and partly because many pieces were originally made in sterling silver, which is a lot cheaper for the faker to work in than gold. Do not buy a poorly finished, blunt-featured Nouveau belt buckle, brooch or pendant. Oddly enough, original Art Nouveau pieces were often handmade from sheets of flat silver, and then soldered together so that the piece had a hollow core; molded reproductions are cast in solid silver and thus are heavier and more substantial in weight than the originals, but in every other way the originals are superior.

There is nothing really wrong with a fine reproduction, and very often, as is the case with museum reproductions, they enable you to wear and enjoy jewelry that you could never find or afford otherwise. But—and it is a big *but*—they should never be passed off as the real thing. It may take a bit of detective work on your part to find out all about the antique piece you plan to buy, but it is fascinating to learn the pedigree of a beautiful time-traveler that ultimately comes to rest with you.

If you do manage to find a piece of antique jewelry you like that is complete, in good condition and not a reproduction, there are still a few questions for you to ask yourself before purchasing it. Styles change, tastes change, and the piece that was once appropriate is not always wearable today. A good example of this is the *lavaliere*, a delicate pendant popular in the early part of the twentieth century, which now has almost no buyers because it simply doesn't look well with today's styles. It is too small in size, too "unimportant," too dainty-looking to compete with today's strong colors and bold fashions. But the lavaliere may come back, and is probably, in terms of gold content and gemstones, a "best buy." But as a general rule, rings, chains, pendants, brooches and bracelets all are more popular because they are still appropriate to today's fashions. And remember that many wonderful old pieces—like many new ones—simply won't be becoming to you. Big bulky beads on a tiny person look ridiculous; long earrings are equally unbecoming to a short neck; small studs get lost in big lobes. So you must ask yourself before you buy any jewelry: Is this becoming? Is it for me?

Old jewelry has to be worn differently than new jewelry, and requires more thought and care. Unlike most modern jewelry, it is unique. It cannot be replaced. So if it breaks or wears out, the repairs should be done only by a jeweler who really loves and understands antiques and doesn't want to replace and restyle and redesign your authentic old treasure into something new and hybrid. The less you repair an old piece the better—and this applies even to old watches. I try not to clean or service my old watches unless they have stopped; most watchmakers don't understand the importance of using old parts on old timepieces, and preferably the *right* old parts from the correct manufacturer. Watches, too, if they are repaired too often, can become a hodgepodge of parts that work, but don't work the way the watch originally was meant to. Even watchbands, when they wear out, should be replaced judiciously. A watch that was meant to have a snakeskin or alligator band should not be fitted out with a twisty bracelet of fake gold! Most important of all, check to see if your old watch has its original buckle, and if it does, make sure that some enterprising jeweler doesn't relieve you of it and replace it with the worthless one that comes with the new band.

Victorian brooches were made to wear on the heavy fabrics of the nineteenth century, and may sag and pull at the light materials of today's clothes. The solution is to put a piece of ribbon behind the pin and "back" it on the inside of your dress to reinforce the hold. Many people take off the old C-catch and long pin so characteristic of nineteenth century pieces and replace them with a modern safety catch, but this is a big mistake. It not only decreases the authenticity and value of your piece, but is not as secure. The old pins, which extended past the edge of the brooch front, were in their own way safety catches. The proper way to fasten them is to weave the pin back and forth through the fabric two or three times, then close the C-clasp and push the protruding point of the pin back into the fabric. This quite effectively anchors the whole brooch, and it will never come loose unless the pinback itself breaks.

Old earrings often were made to enter the ear from behind, and fasten on the front. It's crucial to handle these delicate old survivors with care. Forcing or twisting the thin wires can spell disaster. The proper way to insert these European backs without mangling them or your earlobes is as follows: for the left ear, carefully place the middle finger of your right hand over the hole in the front of your left earlobe. Then take the earring in your left hand, with the wire flipped open, and, feeling for the opening of the hole in the back of your earlobe, slowly push the end of the earwire through till you feel it against that middle finger in front. Then push the wire all the way through, and with the first finger and thumb of your left hand firmly but gently snap it shut. You should hear the snap as it closes. If you have a hard time with this, a bit of petroleum jelly or other lubricant on the tip of the wire should help it enter the hole. Don't force the wire, either through your ear or into the closure; it should go easily once it is in the right place. And don't wear the earrings unless you hear that click as they lock, or you may lose them—a tragedy for antique lovers!

Stickpins or hatpins should never be worn without a "clutch"—a tiny bullet-shaped bit of metal with a spring inside that clutches the end of a pin and holds, and that can be bought in any jewelry store or five-and-ten for about a dollar. With a "clutch," the pin can't pull out of the fabric. In fact, even though the old brooch pins are secure, you may want to slip a clutch onto the pin after it's gone through the fabric once or twice, then continue with the hooking and sticking. Be careful that the clutch doesn't push the brooch pin out of alignment or strain it, threatening the life of the hinge. Clutches come in different sizes, so be sure that the one you buy is the right size to hold firmly on your pin.

While we're on the subject of care let's discuss cleaning your jewelry. Whether it is old or new, remember these rules: always clean gently; do less than you think, not more; and when in doubt, do nothing.

Most jewelers have a terrible compulsion to polish old jewelry. If they get it in their hands for even as small a job as tightening a prong they'll immediately want to throw it into their supersonic cleaning gadget and shake it up like a malted. And while this probably won't damage old chains or rings without stones, it is really dangerous to small gems, which may be shaken loose from their fragile old moorings and lost forever. Worse still, jewelers tend to want to buff and polish your gold and silver until it shines like a newly shellacked floor, a treatment that can be compared to putting a beloved old meerschaum pipe through the washer. Old jewelry develops a soft, lovely patina—an almost invisible pattern of light scratches that evoke age, wear and love. Buffing and polishing does away with this patina completely, leaving behind new, naked metal that gleams gaudily. And once the patina is gone, it cannot be put back, except by time. So when you take a piece of old jewelry in for repair, or even for appraisal, make sure you tell your jeweler firmly and specifically that you do not want it cleaned electronically, buffed or shined. And even if he pouts, hold firm!

But this is not to say that you shouldn't clean *dirt* off your jewelry. Soap and water should do the trick in most cases. But there are exceptions. You should not wash jewelry with foiled stones, hair jewelry, lockets with pictures or any other enclosures, ivory in any form (except by wiping off gently with mild soap and a damp cloth), ribbons or cords, or painted (as distinct from enameled) surfaces. You *can* wash nearly everything else, as long as you are careful. Use a soft brush, like an old eyebrow brush, to get into soap-clogged settings, and if simple soap and water don't work, try soaking in dishwashing soap or, even better, shampoo. Do *not* soak pearls, turquoise or opals, all of which can be harmed by soapy water.

Silver and gold without stones can be soaked in an ammonia-water solution for a short time, but brass or worn gold-filled jewelry cannot—it will turn black. You can also buy a professional jewelry soak from your jeweler or a jewelry supply house, but it won't do the job any better than the simple remedies, and will cost quite a bit more.

And of course, when you rinse off your jewelry, be sure that you do it over a small fine strainer, with the sink stopper closed, and don't let the water out of the sink until you've counted your stones and made sure none is missing.

For simple polishing, I recommend a *rouge cloth*, which your jeweler can get for you if you don't have a jewelry supply store handy. A soft cloth impregnated with a gentle abrasive called jeweler's rouge, this will shine your jewelry without scratching it. If, while rubbing and polishing, you ever feel the prongs of a ring or pin catching on the cloth, stop rubbing immediately and take the piece to the jeweler to have the setting checked.

Pearls need special care in cleaning. Never soak them in ordinary jewelry cleaner, or in any strong solution. You can buy a special pearl cleaner at the jewelry store, but simple soap and water, or—even better—a gentle wipe-off with chamois or silk will suffice. See the chapter on pearls for more detailed information on pearl care.

Opals should be soaked overnight in water, or, preferably, a mixture of water and glycerine. An occasional "bath" like this helps them keep their lively look—especially if you don't wear them often and give them the benefit of the oil and moisture from your own skin.

Large transparent stones can be cleaned by the soap and water method and then buffed a bit with a rouge cloth or a bit of silk. Some people like to soak or rub them with alcohol, but I don't find that this is any better than soap and water or—in the event that they are very dirty—ammonia and water. Diamonds, especially, attract grease, so if you do your dishes with your diamonds on, you'll want to soak them more frequently and, from time to time during the day, give them a bit of a buff on your clothing. This is a good habit to get into, because it not only keeps you in intimate touch with your jewelry, but lets you know immediately if a loose prong is catching against the fabric of your dress. Many a gem has been saved from disaster by a timely "catch."

Of course you should handle your jewelry gently and not drop it or toss it carelessly into a handbag or jewelry box. Even the hardest stones can chip, and the soft ones can scratch, so the best way to take care of them is to put each piece of jewelry in a separate box or compartment of your jewelry box, or, failing that, at least into a small, separate plastic bag. Certain stones, such as pearls, opals and ivory have to "breathe" a little, so plastic is not good for them, and they would do better in cloth or paper boxes. Remember, too, that harder material scratches softer—so keep your precious stones away from more fragile ones, as well as from the soft surfaces of gold and silver.

Some people have difficulty wearing gold chains because the chemistry of their systems causes a reaction to the metal—not the gold, but the alloy—turning their skin or clothing black. A chain or locket without pearls or turquoise can be sprayed lightly with hairspray from time to time, which will probably solve the problem.

146

Let me leave you with this thought: the new jewels of today are the antique heirlooms of tomorrow—and if you take care of all your jewelry and pass it on in as good condition as when it came to you, it will continue to have value and give pleasure for many years.

Costume and
Collectibles

The term "costume jewelry" is generally taken to mean jewelry that is not too expensive, made from modest materials and is more a fashion accessory or fad than a keepsake or a work of art.

Some costume jewelry is just for fun and very fleeting, like the glowing plastic "neon" tubes worn by teenagers or the glittery stars and hearts recently worn like antennae by New Yorkers. Sometimes these whimsical adornments are so reminiscent of a period and so much fun to wear that their popularity lasts long after the fad is over, and they become collectible and collected by jewelry lovers years—even centuries—later. An example of this might be the Mickey Mouse watches, the modest beetles and bugs of the Victorian period, or the plastic five-and-ten Art Deco jewelry that is sought-after today.

But costume jewelry has a serious side, too. Since earliest times, when glass was used in place of gems, or bone stood in for ivory, it has represented man's earnest and occasionally inspired attempts to imitate the real thing. The beautiful, carefully hand-cut pastes of the eighteenth century were costume jewelry, as were the delicate cut-steel parures that glittered under candlelight like diamonds. In

1813, during the Franco-Prussian war, Prussian women donated their precious gold jewelry to the war fund and their grateful government reciprocated with iron jewelry inscribed *"Gold gab ich fur Eisen"* ("I gave gold for iron"). Rare and costly today, this iron jewelry, which looks like beautiful black lace, is sought after by collectors all over the world—but in its time it was merely a special kind of costume jewelry. In the eighteenth century, James Tassie, a talented artist and inventor, became famous for simulating ancient cameos and intaglios in molded glass. After Tassie had passed on his secret process to his nephew, and other, less talented imitators had imitated *him*, these Tassies and Tassie copies became rare and valuable as well. In their time they, too, were costume jewelry.

As recently as the fifties and sixties, chunky plastic bracelets and glass novelty jewelry was sold in the five-and-ten for pennies. That this jewelry has a certain "look"—a period quality that's different from the same kind of inexpensive machine-made jewelry sold today. "Kitsch" collectors think it's fun to wear it, and so flea market dealers can sell collectible fifties and sixties junk jewelry for a hefty profit.

Even more collectible and desirable are the earlier plastics, which are being collected not only by campy youngsters but by serious jewelry lovers and those interested in history. Jewelry is a fascinating barometer of civilizations and cultures, and this early plastic jewelry in particular tells a great deal about the lifestyles and personalities of the people who wore it.

But not all plastic jewelry is "in." The "Deco" look—opaque, bright in color, often embellished with fruit, flower or animal motifs—is the one most desired by dealers and buyers. Its clunky, chunky charm and funny innocence appeal to those of us who abhor today's lean, mechanized culture. And while the people of the Depression period who made and wore this jewelry probably did not think of themselves as innocent, hindsight lends charm to history—and this "Deco-look" plastic now sells for soaring prices, especially considering the fact that it is not "real" jewelry.

If you are interested in old plastic, you should learn what distinguishes the different varieties that were used. All plastic is rather light and warm to the touch, and is easy to recognize. Since plastic is a resinous material molded under heat and pressure, there are usually mold marks on all but the best hand-finished pieces. The first plastic to be invented was *celluloid*, in 1865. Made from natural cellulose, celluloid was used to imitate ivory and amber, and in other jewelry toilet articles and toys as well. But it is highly flammable, and was soon replaced by *safety celluloid*, which, when set afire, burns slowly and emits a sour, vinegary odor. Both kinds of celluloid will soften if they come in contact with acetone, so you can test them by applying nail polish remover inconspicuously with a toothpick to see if the surface is affected.

Polystyrene is a vinyl, usually clear plastic that can be dyed any color. It is used for imitation gems, beads and the cores of imitation pearls. It is very light, and will soften in contact with a bit of benzene.

Acrylic is a plastic that looks like glass, and can be made in any color, transparent or opaque. Like polystyrene, it is used to imitate gemstones or beads, and, like celluloid, can be damaged by acetone. Plexiglas, an acrylic, is often used in costume jewelry.

Bakelite is another early plastic. First produced in 1909, it is a bit harder than the others, and is usually opaque, rather dull and rubbery-looking. It turns yellowish with age and is not very pretty, but it was often used for those chunky Deco pins and bracelets collected and worn today.

Casein is a plastic made from the protein in milk, and has been used to imitate tortoise, amber and ivory. When this plastic is burned it smells like hot milk, and when touched with a bit of nitric acid it turns yellow.

Nylon, too, is used for jewelry. Made from coal tar and ammonia, it is extremely tough, light and durable, but it tends to fade in strong sunlight, and dissolves in acids.

Some costume jewelry is so well-designed and executed that it develops a serious following of its own, and is worn and collected with as much pleasure as the real thing. "Designer" costume jewelry, with names like Trifari, Coro or the earlier Eisenberg, Weiss, Regency or Hattie Carnegie are to costume jewelry what Tiffany, Cartier, Bulgari and Van Cleef and Arpels are to real gems and gold.

Designer costume is usually characterized by well-cut "stones" made of glass, careful finishing and even hand-detailing. The metals really look like gold, platinum or silver and, particularly in evening light, could easily be mistaken for fine jewelry. Designer costume can be expensive, too, and it's not unusual that in a big department store this kind of jewelry can outprice some of the real thing.

These days, designer jewelry comes to the rescue when wealthy people don't want to wear their showy real jewels to a fancy party. As mentioned, often jewelry owners actually have costume copies made of their precious gems, and wear the stand-ins while the genuine articles snuggle safely in the vault.

Ethnic or peasant jewelry of various kinds also ranks as costume—and this would include things like glass trade beads, Scandinavian folk jewelry, African and Near Eastern amulets and beads and the like. Most of what is on the market today has been changed and recombined, but this kind of jewelry is often passed from hand to hand and altered by each owner, so completeness and originality of all the separate elements in the whole is not as important in, for example, a string of Afghanistan beads that might include lapis, low-grade silver, coral and even glass as it would be in a necklace of Victorian amber. The main criteria is that the materials themselves be pleasingly put together and that the piece have *some* unity, perhaps of age or origin, or perhaps even just a pleasing unity of design.

Ethnic jewelry can be exceedingly good-looking—and expensive. Beads or elements that are made of materials like lapis, ivory, amber or silver will drive the price of the piece up; also, large pieces, which the dealers like to call "important," are generally more costly than small ones. This is one area, though, where matching in size and color has practically no meaning; a clever designer will string all kinds of things onto a strand with no regard at all for matching, and somehow make them all look good. If you're buying, the main criterion is taste. But the finishing should be reasonably good; beads should be tightly and carefully strung and finished off with a good clasp (*not* strung on nylon fishline, which is strong and lasts forever, but never looks good because it hangs awkwardly, and eventually pulls apart at the knots). Silver pieces should not be dented or broken, ivory should not be cracked, and overall the whole piece should be well-balanced, becoming and pleasing to wear. Ethnic earrings are often too heavy for our more delicate earlobes, and can actually pull them out of shape if worn too long and too often. Low-grade silver, which is often used in this kind of adornment, will *not* polish up well, no matter what the dealer who wants to sell it to you says, and sometimes it is not really even silver at all, but white metal. "Old" trade beads are often brand-new, big "amber" beads are often *ambroid* (fused powdered amber) or *copal* (a resinlike substance that is much softer, gummier-feeling and not nearly as beautiful as amber). Since large coral beads are very expensive today, sometimes plastic or glass is substituted for real coral, and bone is often identified as ivory. What it all comes down to is this: if you really want to know what is on your string of "ethnic" beads, or what your "primitive" ring or pin is made of, you will have to learn a little about how to identify materials, and trust yourself—not the seller—who may not know as much as you do.

Occasionally there is that fabulous find: a piece of primitive jewelry that comes through time *complete*—all the elements matched or strung just as they were intended—and that piece, whether it's from Africa or China or South America, will be rare, precious and, of course, expensive.

Craft jewelry, made by hand from nonprecious materials like wood, clay, aluminum, brass, shell and glass is also classified as costume, though often the work is very detailed and beautiful, and the pieces are worthy of being worn to the finest event. Craft jewelry, too, can be very expensive, since it often represents many hours of time and thought, but it rarely has any resale value unless the craftsman or woman is well known. If you are buying craft jewelry, remember this. Whatever its makeup, craft jewelry should be becoming, tough enough to stand up under reasonable wear, comfortable and well-balanced. The colors should be permanent and waterproof, the workmanship professional. Pay special attention to details, like findings; often craft brooches with beautiful fronts have cheap, pasted-on pins on the back, which crack off long before the piece has lived a full life. Craft earrings, too, can have glued-on backs that break off, or earwires made of base metal. If you have pierced ears, you really shouldn't put any metal through them except gold or heavy gold-filled. Other metals may irritate your skin.

Cleaning and caring for costume jewelry can be difficult. Sometimes it's hard to identify the many different materials used, and if you don't know the composition of a plastic, for instance, it's best to play it safe and use only mild soap and water. Rhinestones and glittery pastes should never be immersed; the metal may rust and discolor, and if the stones are backed with foil or colored paper, a water bath will ruin them. Often rhinestones or glass fake gems are painted on the back with gold or colored paint. This thin coating improves their look while it lasts, but it may soon peel off and it's really not possible to replace it satisfactorily. When my children were young, they kept a treasure box of fake stones that they collected from all the costume jewelry in the family that had seen its day. Then, when a still-usable piece of jewelry lost a stone or two, the children would supply it from the box. Costume is much less sturdy than real jewelry, and I suggest this "treasure box" approach as a way to keep recycling useful pieces. You can also add clasps to the collection, and old beads, particularly "spacers"—small gold- or silver-colored or contrasting beads that separate the larger elements in a necklace.

Marcasite jewelry has been popular since the ancient Greeks, but we tend to think of it as Art Deco, because it was especially popular in the twenties and thirties. Real marcasite is iron sulphide, and is seldom used in jewelry; instead, iron pyrite, or fool's gold is usually substituted. In early marcasite jewelry the settings might be made of real silver, but today the material used is often common white metal, so look for a "sterling" mark on your marcasite pieces; it is one indication—though not a conclusive one—that your piece may be Deco. Another characteristic of fine older marcasite jewelry is that each iron pyrite crystal was carefully set just like a gemstone. In new marcasite jewelry or "repro" old jewelry, the stones are often glued in, and the first hard wear or contact with water is likely to leave your marcasite piece as holey as swiss cheese. In very old maracasite jewelry, from the eighteenth century, for example, the stones might actually have "rubover" settings— that is, the metal around the crystal is carefully worked up by the craftsmen to hold the stone flush, without prongs or "beads." But this antique marcasite is rare and usually expensive. More common in antique shops is old cut-steel jewelry or shoe buckles that look very similar to marcasite from the front, but can be distinguished from the back by tiny rivets holding each bit of faceted steel in place.

Genuine twenties and thirties marcasite jewelry, set in sterling and mounted with prongs, can be washed or soaked in soapy water just like fine jewelry. But white-metal mountings and pasted-in stones will discolor and fall apart from the same treatment. So be sure to examine your marcasite carefully before you try to clean it. In any case, it should be carefully dried afterwards, and any loose prongs tightened. A very useful addition to your treasure box is any stray marcasite that happens to fall out of an old piece; even in the most carefully crafted marcasite pieces, you should be prepared to lose a stone occasionally.

Because it is iron, marcasite tends to rust—as does cut steel, if you're lucky enough to find it. The best way to prevent rusting is to dry the piece carefully after washing (if you must wash it) and subject it to a small amount of heat—a radiator top, for example. Then oil it very lightly with nonsticky oil to coat the surface. Never wash cut steel unless it is so dirty that it would simply be unwearable otherwise. Once rust gets into these pieces, it is almost impossible to remove. I have never found any substance that will successfully de-rust them without hurting the pieces themselves.

Probably the best way to clean the varied and sometimes cantankerous materials in costume jewelry comes to me from my cleaning lady, who claims that she regularly takes a soft paintbrush to them and simply dusts them off.

A Jewelry Glossary

I thought it would be helpful, before closing this book, to include a list of the words and phrases that you will hear as you buy, collect, invest in and wear jewelry. Some of these terms might already be familiar to you; some of them are specific to the jewelry business, but are essential if you're interested in making a wise investment; and all of them will pop up at some time if you really like jewelry and make it part of your life.

Abrasive Any material that is used to grind or polish metal or to cut, facet or polish stones. It may come in the form of powders, impregnated papers or cloths (such as sandpaper or rouge cloth), or grease combinations. Its hardness is measured on the Mohs scale, and the various gems are polished by grits made from materials that are at least as hard, sometimes harder; sapphires and rubies are polished with corundum powder, diamonds can be cut only with diamonds. Other abrasives used on jewelry include emery, pumice, oilstone, powdered garnet, rottenstone, diatomite, putty powder (tin oxide), rouge and carborundum (silicon carbide).

Acetone This is the colorless liquid which is a prime ingredient in most nail polish removers. It softens cellulose plastics, and can be used (carefully!) to identify them.

Acid Testing (of metals) Many jewelers will offer to test gold, silver or platinum for you to determine its authenticity. The method they usually use is called *acid* or *touchstone testing*.

In this procedure, the metal is first rubbed on a dark basalt or very dense ceramic *touchstone*, where it leaves a mark, or *streak*. If gold is the metal being tested, next to this streak the jeweler makes a similar mark from his set of *gold needles*, of which each pointed finger is tipped with a different karat gold. Now the jeweler applies a few drops of *nitric acid* to the streaks, usually drawing the acid along both marks at the same time. The rate at which the marks fade tells him the karat of gold and, if he is skilled, what the gold is alloyed with. A comparison of the original streak with the identified karat of the gold needle confirms the diagnosis. If the streak is yellow, the alloy is copper; if it is white, it may be silver, nickel or tin. If it fades immediately the gold content is so slight that there may be none at all. This means that the acid has attacked and "eaten" the alloy; gold, the "noble" metal, remains untouched by acid. If the streak fades slowly but completely, it is probably about 14 karat; if it never completely fades, leaving a yellow "bloom" on the stone, it is 18 karat or better. By comparing it to the known karat of the gold needles, it is easy to judge the karat of the gold.

If the streak remains after the nitric acid, touch it again with *hydrochloric acid*. (Many jewelers do not do this second step.) The two acids will mingle to form *aqua regia*, which attacks most streaks not affected by the nitric acid alone. Now if a white film develops, the streak is lead; if it dissolves quickly, the streak is aluminum; if it dissolves slowly it could be stainless steel, platinum, high quality *palladium* (see below), or high-karat white gold. Following this, if the acid is absorbed with a bit of white blotting paper, its *color* can be seen. If the stain is strongly brown, the metal is palladium; weak brown indicates white gold mixed with palladium; greenish yellow identifies stainless steel or white gold alloyed with nickel. If aqua regia doesn't affect the streak at all, then the metal you have is pure platinum.

Now, for the final test: if, after step two, you are still not sure if the meal left is white gold alloyed with nickel or with stainless steel, make a new streak, warm the touchstone just a bit, and apply hydrochloric acid. Stainless steel will disappear; white gold or nickel will leave a mark. Now your metal is identified—unless it is silver.

The test for silver is slightly different. It can be done with a touchstone, using a streak and a solution of silver nitrate (2 grams dissolved in 30 ccs water) plus a drop of nitric acid. This will not dissolve a streak made by sterling silver, but will dissolve low-grade silver (below 900/1000 parts). A simpler test is made with a special silver-test solution, bought in a jewelry store or jewelry supply house, that will turn bright red when in contact with silver. However, this solution leaves a bright spot on the piece tested that is hard to polish away, so it should always be used in an inconspicuous area.

Some jewelers simply drop acid on gold, without using the stone, and some don't even own needles. What I've described here is the complete and proper way. If your jeweler does this, he is a painstaking and precise craftsman, and his diagnosis is to be trusted.

Some jewelers, unworthy of the name, actually *file* gold and precious metals to determine what's inside, afraid that the piece might be base metal covered with gold, or gold filled. It is true that the touchstone testing really only determines what's on the outside of a piece, but filing is destructive, and I don't feel that it can be justified, ever—even in the pursuit of gold.

Adularescence This refers to the bluish white sheen of

moonstone, the result of light reflecting from the inner layers of the gem.

Agate A gem variety of quartz that comes in many forms: banded, with circular patterns, with ferny markings, with snowflakes or polka dots and in many colors, all of which have their own names (onyx: black; carnelian: orange red; etc.). Agate is not crystalline and very rarely transparent. Its Mohs scale hardness is 7. Agate has been used in jewelry since ancient times, and, though there is plenty of it available, it has always been much prized. Most ancient seals were made of agate, and, in fact, it is still used for that purpose. Tumbled agates of various colors are popular at rock shows and craft fairs as inexpensive yet beautiful keepsakes. For more information, see the chapter on SEMIPRECIOUS STONES.

À Jour An open-backed setting that allows light to shine through a stone, thus making it open "to the day."

Alexandrite A semiprecious stone which changes color and looks green in daylight, red in artificial light. See the chapter on SEMIPRECIOUS STONES.

Alloy A combination of two or more metals. Usually the word "alloy" is taken to mean the less valuable metal that is combined with the more precious one (gold, silver or platinum). The word is probably from the French "*à la loi*" (according to the law), inasmuch as the alloying of precious metals has, since earliest times, been under the careful scrutiny of the government.

Gold and silver are alloyed before they are used in jewelry because they are too soft to wear well without the addition of other metals. Platinum is also alloyed to give it better workability. The proportion of alloy to precious metal is regulated in most countries, and in many countries the gold or silver must be marked with the correct proportions to be commercially sold. Platinum needs only a very small amount of alloy added, perhaps 5 percent, and is often unmarked.

For more information, see the chapter on GOLD, or SILVER.

Almandine Garnet A purplish red garnet that was very popular in the nineteenth century, and considered a finer stone than the more common red, or *pyrope* garnet. See SEMIPRECIOUS STONES.

Aluminum A very light silver-colored metal that is sometimes used in modern jewelry. Aluminum is also used sometimes to alloy with gold in an effort to simulate platinum.

Amazonite A greenish blue feldspar sometimes used for beads or cabochons in jewelry. It does *not* come from the Amazon, but from the United States, Brazil, Russia and South Africa.

Amber A very light, soft (2½ on the Mohs scale) fossil resin that has been used in jewelry since earliest times. Its creation goes back to the Oligocene period, when the sap of giant conifer trees solidified, sometimes still carrying the remains of insects or plants. Over the centuries this resin was buried and then washed (or mined) out of the soil. The Greek word for amber was *elektron*, because of its peculiar capacity, when electrified by rubbing, to pick up small bits of light material. The word by which it is known today comes from the Arabic *anbar*, meaning ambergris (no connection with amber) probably because it was often found washed up on the seashore. See SEMIPRECIOUS STONES.

Amethyst Transparent purple quartz, often used as a gemstone. In Greek, *amethystos* means "not drunk," and amethysts were believed to prevent drunkenness—perhaps because their color resembles that of grapes. See SEMIPRECIOUS STONES.

Antique Jewelry Technically, any jewelry more than one hundred years old is considered to be "antique." But in practice, this term is loosely used to include much more recent jewelry, including: Art Nouveau jewelry, which dates back to the latter quarter of the nineteenth and the early years of the twentieth century; Art Deco, which flourished in the twenties and thirties; and even fifties jewelry, which is sometimes incorrectly termed "antique" by dealers because it sounds so much better than "secondhand," or "collectible."

Aqua Regia A mixture of nitric and hydrochloric acids used to test gold and platinum. It is also known as *royal water* because it is the only liquid known to dissolve the "noble" metal, gold.

Aquamarine A transparent blue green beryl (hardness: 7½–8) used as a gemstone.

For more information, see the chapter on SEMI-PRECIOUS STONES.

Arkansas Diamond A misnomer for a clear crystal quartz.

Art Nouveau For roughly twenty years, from 1890 to 1910, the Art Nouveau style, a romantic flowing look that was based on asymmetry, curves and the natural forms of flowers, leaves, insects and dreaming women's faces, flourished in all the arts. Cabochons and rounded forms were popular, as were silvery or iridescent finishes. In addition to silver, opals, moonstones and pearls, semiprecious and even flawed and irregular stones were popular.

See ANTIQUE JEWELRY.

Asterism This refers to the "star" effect of star rubies or star sapphires.

Aventurine A kind of quartzite that has "spangles" of mica or iron, aventurine is also imitated (almost better than the original) in glass, and called *aventurine glass*, or, more popularly, "Goldstone."

Azurite A soft (Mohs scale: 3½–4) blue stone usually found in combination with malachite, this is attractive in jewelry, but too easily worn down. It is sometimes mistaken for turquoise, which is harder and more valuable.

Baguette A narrow rectangle cut, usually used for small diamonds that flank a center, larger stone.

Bakelite An early plastic.

See the chapter on COSTUME AND COLLECTIBLES.

Ball Catch Another name for the round safety catch on the backs of most modern brooches.

Bangle A stiff (nonflexible) bracelet, usually round or oval, worn at the wrist.

Baroque A polished stone or a pearl of irregular shape.

Base Metal Any metal other than gold, silver or platinum.

Basse-Taille A type of enamel.

See the chapter MORE ABOUT METALS.

Beads Everyone knows what a bead is, so it hardly needs to be defined here. Perhaps not as well known is the fact that beads were probably man's earliest form of adornment. There isn't a material around that hasn't been drilled, bored or strung by one civilization or another, either in patterns, combinations, graded by size or graduated, just as we moderns do today.

Beryl A mineral family with many notable members, including emeralds (green), aquamarine (blue–green), heliodor (yellow) and morganite (pink).

See THE PRECIOUS GEMS and THE SEMIPRECIOUS STONES.

Birthstones It is an ancient custom to link birthdays (or more accurately, birth months) with gemstones. The origin of this idea is lost in folklore and magic, but the stones generally associated with date of birth are the following:

JANUARY	GARNET
FEBRUARY	AMETHYST (or ONYX)
MARCH	AQUAMARINE (or BLOODSTONE)
APRIL	DIAMOND (or ROCK CRYSTAL)
MAY	EMERALD (or CHRYSOPRASE)

JUNE	PEARL (or MOONSTONE)
JULY	RUBY (or CARNELIAN)
AUGUST	PERIDOT (or SARDONYX)
SEPTEMBER	SAPPHIRE (or LAPIS LAZULI)
OCTOBER	OPAL (or TOURMALINE)
NOVEMBER	TOPAZ (or CITRINE)
DECEMBER	TURQUOISE (or BLUE ZIRCON)

Biwa Pearls Beautiful cultured pearls from Lake Biwa, Japan. Biwas have a special luster that distinguishes them from other cultureds; also, unlike other cultureds they are all nacre (rather than shell or clay), they are started with a bit of tissue that is absorbed as the pearl is formed.

Bloodstone Chalcedony, which is of dark greenish color, spotted with small red marks, like drops of blood.
See SEMIPRECIOUS STONES.

Blue-White Diamond This is really a misnomer. In an effort to describe a perfectly clear diamond without tinges of yellow (or other colors), jewelers coined the term blue-white to mean "perfectly clear." In fact, the correct term for this is "of the first water," or "of the finest, or first river." A diamond which is "bluish" in color is actually less favored than a pure "white" (a misnomer, too!) clear one.

Bombay Bunch A selection of pearls threaded onto silk, but not ready for wearing. This is how pearls are exported from Bombay to other countries—hence the term.

Brass An alloy of copper and zinc, often used as the interior metal over which gold is pressed for "gold filled" jewelry.
See GOLD.

Brazilian Emerald Not actually an emerald at all, but a green tourmaline. Beware also of *Brazilian rubies*, which are really topaz, and *Brazilian sapphires*, which are really blue tourmalines. In general, don't hesitate to question any gemstone name preceded by a mysterious "origin" name. If the answer to "What is a Colombian emerald?" is "An emerald mined in Colombia" (which is correct), you have lost nothing. If the answer to "What is a Brazilian emerald?" turns out to be a shamefaced "...A green tourmaline," you'll be glad you asked.

Brilliant A diamond faceted in the brilliant cut.
   See THE PRECIOUS GEMS: DIAMONDS.

Briolette A tear-shaped stone, usually a diamond, faceted front and back. A briolette is usually used as a pendant, or for earrings.

Brooch A pin, or piece of jewelry that is worn attached to clothing. "Brooch" is a term more commonly used by the British, but I use it in this book to save confusion, since "pin" also refers to the long, narrow pointed piece of metal that pins a brooch onto you. "Brooch" sounds rather snooty in ordinary conversation, so avoid using it in sentences like "The baby's diapers need a safety brooch!"

Buffing Fine light polishing of metal or stones.

Button Pearls Pearls with a round top and flat base.
   See the chapter on PEARLS.

Cabochon The oldest style of gemcutting, rounded on top, flat on the bottom. Star stones are still cut in this manner, as are opaque stones like turquoise and lapis, and sometimes flawed or off-color stones which still are beautiful enough for jewelry. *Chatoyant* stones, like cat's eye and moonstone, are nearly always cut cabochon, and red garnets cut this way are called *carbuncles*.

California Cat's Eye Like *Brazilian*, the adjective *California*, when it precedes the name of a gem, can hide a multitude of sins. *California cat's eye* is really fibrous serpentine with only the faintest chatoyancy; *California iris* is a misnomer for kunzite; *California jade* is really idocrase; *California lapis* is blue quartz, and on and on. Be careful!

Cameo A stone or shell on which a design is carved in *relief* (that is, the background is lower than the subject, as distinct from an *intaglio*, like a seal, in which the design is carved into and below the background). Ancient cameos were of stone or shell, and these two materials are still used, though shell is far the more common nowadays. Cameo making is an exact and delicate art, and skilled masters are rare today. Real experts can date a cameo not only by the material used but by the subject matter and style. But today, in Italy, craftsmen still imitate the old cameos, and new ones can be bought that are as beautiful and as detailed as the ancient ones—if you are willing to hunt them down and pay the price. The hallmark of a fine cameo is good use of the variations in the material, the opaqueness or translucence, the light or dark bands of color, deep relief carving and, in the best work, *undercutting*, a technique by which the subject seems almost to stand away from the background. The delicacy of carving is important, too; a good cameo should look even more beautiful under a magnifying glass than it does to the naked eye.

Other materials are used for cameos and intaglios, such as mother-of-pearl, lapis and coral, and the Chinese were skilled in using amber and lacquer—but shell is really the most popular and the most common.

Canary Diamond A yellow diamond.

Carat 1. The unit of weight for precious stones and pearls (though pearls are also expressed in grains; see the chapter on PEARLS). One carat (which is said to have derived from the weight of a carob seed) equals one fifth of a gram.

2. English spelling of *karat*, the measure of the proportion of gold to alloy. See chapter on GOLD.

Carbonado A rare black form of diamond which comes from Brazil. It is not especially valued for jewelry, but is highly regarded in industry for its toughness.

Carbuncle A red cabochon garnet.

Carnelian Agate of a red or red-orange color.

Casting A way of reproducing an object by creating a *mold*— an outer covering which fits the original *model* perfectly— then taking the original out, and pouring a liquid (in the case of jewelry, liquid metal) into the mold. When the liquid cools and the mold is removed, there is a new object formed exactly like the old one.

Casting, though widely practiced in jewelry, is not considered as beautiful as hand crafting, and handmade jewelry is always more expensive than comparable cast pieces.

Cat's Eye Yellowish brown chatoyant crysoberyl. See the chapter on SEMIPRECIOUS STONES for more details.

Celluloid The earliest plastic used in jewelry. See COSTUME AND COLLECTIBLES for more about plastics.

Chalcedony Agate. Chalcedony is massy, nontransparent and often used in carvings or for beads.

Chasing A method of decorating jewelry in which the embellishment is done from the front of the piece. *Repoussé*, a method of working from the inside, is the opposite of chasing. These words imply work that is done in *relief*; *engraving*, also done from the front, merely means cutting a pattern into the metal.

Chatham Emerald A synthetic emerald.

Chatoyancy A streak of light that flashes when certain stones are moved back and forth, like cat's eyes.

Cherry Opal Common red Mexican opal.

Choker A short necklace, usually about fifteen inches long.

Citrine Transparent yellow quartz, sometimes confused with—but not nearly as valuable as—topaz.

Coral The skeleton of a sea creature, the coral polyp, that is sometimes used in jewelry. See SEMIPRECIOUS STONES.

Corundum The mineral family whose two most famous members are *sapphires* and *rubies*. For more details, see the chapter on these gems.

Crown The part of a faceted gemstone that is above the *waist*, or *girdle*.

Crystal 1. The orderly form some minerals naturally take, this depending on their atomic structure. A mineral that has large, symmetrical crystals and is clear and transparent is often used as a gemstone.

2. Clear crystalline quartz, or rock crystal is often called simply *crystal*. Glass, too, is sometimes referred to as *crystal*.

Culet The small bottom facet at the base of a brilliant or old mine-cut diamond, or other faceted gemstone.

Cultured Pearl See the chapter on PEARLS for an explanation of how real pearls are artificially induced in real oysters.

Cushion Cut Stones cut with a squarish outline and rounded corners, like a cushion.

Damascening The ancient art of producing a "watered" pattern in steel, or, in more modern terms, of inlaying gold or silver into other metals.

De Beers Consolidated Mines, Ltd. The huge South African conglomerate that controls virtually all of the production, distribution and pricing of world diamonds.

For a more detailed discussion, see the chapter on DIAMONDS.

Demantoid Garnet Beautiful green garnets, rarely seen today, much beloved in nineteenth-century jewelry.

Diamond The hardest of gemstones.

See chapter on DIAMONDS.

Dichroic The capacity to show two shades of the same color, depending on the axis along which a stone is viewed. Gems which are dichroic are also *doubly refractive* (that is, they split the light that enters them into two separate rays), though not all doubly refractive stones are dichroic. In faceting a dichroic stone, a cutter must carefully decide which axis will yield the richest, best color and orient his cutting to take advantage of that quality.

Doublet A fake, really, since it consists of one thin layer of

167

a real gemstone, perhaps opal, cemented to one or more layers of a worthless material. The aim is to convince the hapless buyer that the whole "sandwich" is real. When there are three layers, the stone is called a *triplet*; it is every bit as fake.

Double Refraction Splitting up light passing through a gemstone into two rays. This means that if you look at a plain pencil line through a gem that is doubly refractive— like a ruby—you will see two lines; if you look through a singly refractive stone—such as a garnet—only one line will appear. This is one method, though only one, of distinguishing a ruby from its more modest kinsman, garnet.

Electroplating A process by which a very thin layer of gold or silver is deposited electrically on base metal. Electroplated jewelry is not really wearable, since the gold or silver will scuff off, leaving the bare base metal visible.

Electrum In ancient times electrum was popular as material for jewelry, and was described by the historian Pliny as one part silver to five of gold. This alloy occurred naturally in the gold-bearing mines of Asia Minor. Nowadays more or less the same alloy is called *white gold*.

Emerald A beryl of fine dark green color, the rarest of the precious stones.

Enameling The art of fusing powdered colored glass with heat and then cooling it to coat the surface of an underlying metal.

Engagement Rings In ancient Rome, when young lovers were betrothed, the bride's father promised her to the groom in a ceremony involving the exchanging of rings; gold could only be worn in those days by the privileged, so a ring of iron, called the *anulus pronubis*, was given instead by the groom to his bride. By the third century A.D. this ring was made of gold, and familiar symbols decorated the betrothal ring: clasped hands, lovers' knots and sentimental inscriptions. In time this betrothal ring became a wedding ring, the symbol of the marital contract, and another ring, the engagement ring, took its place as the appropriate gift for troth-pledging. But this took almost a thousand years.

In the intervening centuries, the custom of giving some kind of ring as a love token or marriage token continued in different forms. Many of these rings survive today, with the same symbols inscribed on the inside or outside: clasped hands, lovers' knots and amorous sentiments. But it wasn't until the nineteenth century that the custom of wearing both a wedding and engagement ring took hold. Queen Victoria's engagement ring, a token of love from her adored Albert, was in the form of a snake with its tail in its mouth—a symbol of eternal life known as an *oroborus*. In the mid-nineteenth century pearl engagement rings were popular, but by the end of the century diamonds took their place as the most romantic engagement symbol, perhaps because the De Beers empire (consolidated in South Africa at about the same time) advertised that the diamond was the most enduring and pure of gemstones, really the only proper gift when declaring one's love.

Lately new gemstones—or rather, old ones—have been gaining popularity as engagement tokens: pearls (always valued as a symbol of purity and love), antique rings of all kinds and sapphires, the choice of the Prince of Wales to Lady Diana.

And while the *kind* of ring given has varied through the centuries, the custom of *giving a ring* to plight one's troth seems so universal a custom that jewelers need not tremble; it looks as if lovers will be buying each other *something* till the end of time.

Engraving Incising a linear design in metal or gemstones with a sharp tool. This technique goes back to the third millennium B.C. when tools of flint, copper and bronze were used by ancient craftsmen to engrave sheets of gold.

Nowadays most engraving is done by machine, but hand engraving is still practiced as an art, and hand-engraved initials or sentiments are still popular on jewelry.

Etching Decorating metal, glass or gemstones by cutting patterns into them with acids. The most common method is to coat the surface of the material with waxlike substance, then cut the design into the wax with a sharp tool. When acid is applied to the entire surface, only the cut-through pattern is eaten into, or etched. Etching can also be used on an entire surface to texture it or produce a surface pattern.

The acid most often used on gold is diluted *aqua regia* (a combination of nitric and hydrochloric acid); and on silver, it is nitric acid.

Facet One small flat surface cut into a gemstone.

Fancy Usually a stone of unusual color. This term is especially used for colored diamonds, called *fancy diamonds*, or *fancies*.

Filigree A method involving the working of delicate strands of gold or silver wire into fine lacy patterns. Filigree jewelry dates back to the third millennium B.C., and has been popular in Middle Eastern jewelry throughout history. Craftsmen in these areas still produce silver filigree jewelry for tourists which closely resembles ancient pieces.

Fine When used to describe the precious metals, "fine" means "pure"—that is, "fine gold" or "fine silver" would be pure metal, unalloyed. However, "fine" is also commonly used in jewelry simply to denote condition, or even as a qualitative term: a "fine design," or a "fine emerald" or even a "fine bargain."

Fire The flashes of colored light that are characteristic of some gemstones, most notably diamonds.

First Water A term used in the jewelry business to describe diamonds that are of ultimate clarity and perfectly free of flaws.

Flaws In transparent gemstones, a flaw is any mark or crack or inclusion which mars its utter clarity, thereby detracting from its value. The exception to this rule would be inclusions or structural flaws which actually give the stone its character, such as the structure of the opal, which is responsible for the uneven play of fire in its heart, or the cavities or inclusions that produce the "star" in a star ruby or sapphire. In an emerald, which is almost never entirely free from flaws, the minute inclusions, called *jardin*, are thought to give it character, and unless they cloud it and make it murky, are not really considered to be flaws.

Off-color is also a flaw in many stones: sapphires that are too dark or light, rubies that are too pale or orangy, diamonds that have a yellowish tinge which isn't deep enough to make them *canaries* (a term for yellow fancies), would all be considered less valuable, and therefore flawed. Poor cutting, or chips on the surface of a stone, are also considered to be defects, as are poor proportion in cutting, uneven color or evidence of manipulation of color by heat, dyeing and staining.

Freshwater Pearls Pearls from river mussels.
See the chapter on PEARLS.

Garnet A popular family of semiprecious stones.
See SEMIPRECIOUS STONES for a more complete rundown.

Girdle The widest part of a faceted gemstone. Above the girdle is the *crown*; below, the *pavilion*, or *base*.

Gold Let's let Thomas Hood say it:

> Gold! Gold! Gold! Gold!
> Bright and yellow, hard and cold,
> Molten, graven, hammer'd, and roll'd;
> Heavy to get, and light to hold;
> Hoarded, barter'd, bought, and sold,
> Stolen, borrow'd, squander'd, doled;
> Spurn'd by the young, but hugg'd by the old
> To the very verge of the churchyard mould...!
> (from *Miss Kilmansegg: Her Moral*)

For the facts, see the chapter on GOLD.

Grain A unit of weight for pearls. There are 480 grains to the Troy ounce. One grain equals .25 carats.

Granulation A decoration for gold surfaces of tiny beads attached to the surface to form patterns, lines or a background texture. This technique was used with great skill in ancient Etruscan jewelry, and in Victorian times was imitated and called *Etruscan work*.

Hallmarks Marks or symbols stamped into gold or silver jewelry (or other objects) which tell the karat of gold or quality of silver used, and perhaps the maker, the country of origin or even the year in which the piece was crafted.

Hardness An important quality of a gemstone. See MOHS SCALE, below.

Heliodor Golden yellow transparent beryl.

Heliotrope Another name for bloodstone.

Hematite Opaque blue-black iron oxide, used as a gemstone and admired for its brilliant luster.

Herkimer Diamond Not diamond at all, but rock crystal from Herkimer County in upstate New York.

Honan Jade Misleading name for ordinary soapstone.

Hoop The part of the ring worn around the finger, also called the *shank*.

Illusion Setting Developed in the nineteenth century, the illusion setting placed prongs at the corners of a stone, usually a diamond, to give the cunning illusion that the gem was larger than it really was. This setting is still popular, for the same reasons.

Imperial Jade Translucent jade of the finest emerald green color, this rare and magnificent jade is highly and deservedly prized.

Inclusions Small bits of foreign matter trapped within a transparent gemstone, inclusions are usually considered flaws. But they have their value, for they can be the key that unlocks the mystery of a stone's origin, or certifies its genuineness.

Intaglio The opposite of a cameo, an intaglio is a pattern or design cut into the surface of a metal or a gemstone. A seal is an intaglio.

Irradiated Diamonds In 1904, Sir William Crookes experimented with exposing diamonds to radium to change their color. He found that after long exposure, irradiated diamonds turned permanently dark green on the surface, a color more like a tourmaline than the bright apple green of a natural fancy green diamond. These early irradiated diamonds are still radioactive, and if left in a dark box with photographic film for a number of hours, will "fog" the film.

More recently, diamonds have been bombarded with atomic particles to produce green color in yellowish or brownish stones, and then heated to about 800 degrees Centigrade. These diamonds have permanent color, but it is marred by triangular markings which can be detected under a microscope; their radioactivity dies out within a few hours. High-speed electrons and gamma rays can produce aquamarine color in diamonds, but this technique is still experimental. All these irradiated stones can be detected by sophisticated instruments, such as those used by the GIA.

See THE PRECIOUS STONES: DIAMONDS.

Ivory An ancient material from the tusks of elephants used for jewelry and ornaments.

See the chapter on SEMIPRECIOUS STONES.

Jade The most prized gemstone of the Orient, jade has been carved and treasured for more than three thousand years.

See the chapter on SEMIPRECIOUS STONES for more details.

Jadeite Jadeite, or *yu* to the Chinese, is the precious form of jade.

See the chapter on SEMIPRECIOUS STONES.

Jardin The mossy inclusions in the heart of an emerald.

Jasper A reddish brown or yellowish quartz, originally a kind of petrified wood.

Jump Ring Small O-shaped ring used to connect elements in jewelry.

Karat In America, the term used to define the fineness of gold, or percentage of gold to alloy in any given piece. See GOLD.

Keeper Ring Ring worn to prevent the loss of a more valuable ring, often worn with a wedding ring.

King Cut A recent version of the brilliant cut, featuring 86 facets. It is usually applied to large diamonds.

Kunzite A blue violet stone discovered in California around the turn of the century. See SEMIPRECIOUS STONES.

La Paz Pearls Gray or bronze colored pearls from the waters of Mexico and South America.

Lapis Lazuli A beautiful opaque stone, dark blue with characteristic gold-colored flecks. See SEMIPRECIOUS STONES.

Laxey Diamonds Diamonds cut in a shallow brilliant-cut. The term was probably derived from "lasque diamonds," flat diamonds faceted by Indian cutters.

Locket A pendant that opens up to reveal a picture or keepsake inside.

Lockets go back to about the seventeenth century, when they were popular as containers for religious relics. Some early lockets contained painted miniatures, likenesses of a king, perhaps, or of a loved one. In the nineteenth century lockets were widely used as receptacles for a beloved's hair or even a bit of fabric from their clothing; during the Civil War there was hardly a woman in this country who didn't wear a locket that hid an absent loved one's picture or "pledge." The shapes were generally oval; round lockets became popular a few decades later.

Nowadays lockets are still loved as sentimental gifts, and

174

their shape and general style is still very much like early ones. Human nature—and jewelry—doesn't change much!

Loupe A jeweler's magnifying glass, held up to the eye to examine stones and small objects. A 4X or 5X magnification is sufficient for metal jewelry; 10X is best to view gemstones.

Lucite A kind of plastic. See COSTUME AND COLLECTIBLES.

Luminescence Some gemstones have the property of returning light under certain types of stimulation—including ultraviolet light. This makes it possible for anyone with a "black light" (you can buy one in any rock or hobby shop) to do simple tests that will identify certain gems or distinguish them from synthetics.

Books can—and have—been written about gem luminescence, but a few simple facts might help clarify the use of luminescence in gem identification.

Under an ultraviolet lamp, a natural emerald stays dark; a synthetic emits a bright crimson glow. Diamonds often show a bluish glow (or *fluorescence*); white sapphires, which resemble diamonds, and colorless glass (or pastes), show no color at all. Benitoite, which looks rather like sapphire, glows blue under shortwave ultraviolet; natural sapphires barely respond to it; synthetic sapphires glow green.

If you are seriously interested in identifying stones, an inexpensive longwave/shortwave ultraviolet lamp, and a book which explains how to use it, are good investments.

Luster The surface brilliance of a gem or metal.

Mabe Pearl A half pearl, usually large, usually used for an earring. Another spelling is *Mobe*.

See the chapter on PEARLS.

Magna Cut A modern version of the brilliant cut with 102 facets. This is usually used only with large stones.

Maiden Pearl A pearl newly pulled from the water. Isn't this a lovely term?

Malachite A bright green mineral (copper carbonate) which occurs in bulgy seams rather than crystals *(botryoidal* form) and is banded and opaque. It was widely used for jewelry in the nineteenth century, and is popular these days for beads. Zaire imports poorly rounded but quite charming strands of malachite, and the stone also occurs in the United States, Australia and the Urals.
See SEMIPRECIOUS STONES.

Maori Jade A dark green nephrite jade from New Zealand, usually used for carving "tikis," or primitive talismans.

Marcasite Iron pyrite crystals, used in jewelry of the twenties and thirties, and still popular today.
See COSTUME AND COLLECTIBLES.

Marquise A boat-shaped stone (long pointed oval), usually a diamond.

Matrix The background rock in which a gem is found.

Mélange Diamond term, meaning a group of stones of mixed sizes, all weighing over .25 carats.

Mélée Another diamond term, this one meaning small stones that weigh less than .25 carats.

Melon A popular shape for beads, a long round with ridges from end to end, like a cantaloupe.

Mizpah A word that appears on much nineteenth-century sentimental jewelry, MIZPAH is a biblical name that means "The Lord watch between me and thee, when we are absent one from another."

Mohs Scale Devised in 1822 by Friedrich Mohs, this list of ten materials in order of their hardness is used to help identify minerals. The list is: 1) Talc 2) Gypsum 3) Calcite 4) Fluorspar 5) Apatite 6) Feldspar 7) Quartz 8) Topaz 9) Corundum 10) Diamond. The harder stone will always scratch the softer.

Momme A Japanese unit of weight for pearls.
See the chapter on PEARLS.

Moonstone A softly glowing bluish white gemstone that shimmers with characteristic *adularescence.*
See SEMIPRECIOUS STONES.

Morganite Transparent pink beryl, named after J. P. Morgan.

Moro Coral Dark red coral from Japan.

Mosaic Tiny bits of glass, stone or other brightly colored materials arranged in a recessed background in the form of patterns or pictures so that the whole has a smooth surface. This decorative technique is very old; Roman mosaics still endure, though they graced floors, not jewelry, and in the nineteenth century, in imitation of these ancient mosaics, mosaic jewelry became very popular. It is still made in Greece and Italy, mostly for tourists, very much in the manner of the ancients. The finest mosaics have very small pieces, or *tesserae,* many subtle colors, and a very fine smooth surface, so they look almost like a painting.

Another kind of mosaic popular in the nineteenth century was *pietra dura*—mosaic "puzzles" of stone in which the pieces were various colored semiprecious stones, usually opaque ones, against a background of black onyx.

Moss The inclusions in emeralds which give the gem a murky look.

Mother-of-Pearl The nacreous lining of a shell, also used for jewelry, as well as other decorative objects.

Mutton-Fat Jade Yellowish white jade (nephrite) esteemed highly by the Chinese.

Nacre The substance secreted by pearl-bearing mollusks which, when deposited around an irritant within the shell, creates a pearl.

Natural This is probably self-evident, but the term "natural" when used to describe a gem or pearl means that

177

it is *not* a number of other things: synthetic, fake, imitation, dyed, treated, etc. If you are in doubt of just what "natural" means, *ask*.

Navette Another word for the *marquise* or *boat-shaped* cut.

Nephrite A kind of jade.
See SEMIPRECIOUS STONES.

New Jade A misnomer. New Jade is really *bowenite*, a much softer, much less valuable form of *serpentine*.

New Zealand Greenstone New Zealand or Maori jade.

Nickel Silver Not silver at all, but an alloy of copper, nickel and zinc. The other name for this combination is *German silver*. Nickel silver is not much used now, but is common in inexpensive nineteenth-century jewelry and decorative objects.

Niello A process by which dark metal is inlaid into silver or gold in patterns or pictures. This kind of decoration can be traced back to Roman times, and various recipes have been given for the niello mixture, but it is usually a combination that includes copper, sulphur, silver and lead.

Niello is still being made, primarily in the East.

Nitric Acid The acid used for testing low-karat gold or silver, and, in combination with hydrochloric acid in *aqua regia*, the test for high-karat gold and platinum.

Noble Metal A term used for gold and platinum (and sometimes even for silver) to denote the most precious and resistant metals. Sometimes "noble" gems are referred to; these would most likely be diamonds, sapphires, rubies and emeralds—the most precious, rare and valuable.

Obsidian Natural black glass formed by the cooling of volcanic lava, and sometimes used in jewelry. Obsidian looks like onyx, but it is softer, warmer to the touch and less resistant to wear. It comes from various parts of North and South America, was used by the ancient Aztecs and Mayans, and also occurs in Hawaii, Iceland and Japan.

Occidental A term to watch for; it usually means "fake." For example: an *Occidental diamond* is rock crystal, an *Occidental topaz* is citrine, an *Occidental cat's eye* is quartz and an *Occidental agate* is of poor quality.

Octahedron An eight-sided crystal. Because of its shape, an octahedron, when sawed in half, looks almost like a faceted stone—and indeed, the earliest diamonds were treated this way and set into rings and brooches.

Odontolite A blue fossilized material resembling turquoise. Odontolite is found in the south of France.

Off-Color Used to describe diamonds with a yellowish cast.

Old-Mine Cut Another diamond term. This one describes the old style of brilliant cutting which featured a cushion-shaped stone with a high crown. Old-mine cuts are not as flashingly fiery as more modern cuts, and thus not as highly valued. An otherwise good stone cut in this fashion might bring a slightly lower price than a more modishly cut one. A diamond in the old-mine cut is commonly and affectionately referred to as "an old-miner."

Olive A long bead drilled edge to edge.

Onyx Black agate, occasionally banded with white.
See SEMIPRECIOUS STONES.

Opal A unique gemstone, an oxide of silicon which is remarkable for its milky appearance and the play of many colored fiery dots in its heart.
See SEMIPRECIOUS STONES.

Open Setting A gem setting in which the top and bottom of the stone are open to the light.

Orient The characteristic iridescent luster of fine pearls.

Oriental This word, when used to describe gemstones or pearls, usually means "natural," or "real." But beware; assume nothing! And ask questions!

Oxblood Coral Very valuable coral of deep red color. If you buy it, make sure it isn't dyed!

Palladium A white precious metal used rarely in jewelry. See MORE ABOUT METALS.

Panama Pearls Black or dark blue pearls from the Mexican Gulf.

Paragons Very large, very round real pearls. Also used as a trade name for imitation pearls. Make sure you know exactly what is meant when this term is used!

Parure A matching set, applying to any kind of jewelry. This term is used more often for antique than for modern jewelry.

Paste Basically, glass. Pastes, very high-quality hand-faceted glass stones, were popular in earlier centuries, and were carefully hand-set. They are now collected and worn proudly—not as false gemstones, but as real paste. However, today's glass gems are machine-made and cheaply set; unfortunately, modern paste jewelry usually isn't very exciting.

Pavé Setting A method of setting small stones into metal so that the surface is even, or "paved."

Pavilion The facets of a gemstone that lie below the girdle.

Pearls Pearls are such an important part of the world of jewelry that a whole chapter could be devoted to them—and has been. Please see PEARLS.

Pendeloque A pear-shaped drop, faceted in the brilliant cut.

Peridot A yellowish green transparent gemstone, the gem variety of olivine. Peridot is soft (6½ on the Mohs scale), with a rather greasy luster. It was immensely popular in the nineteenth century, somewhat less so in the twentieth.

See SEMIPRECIOUS STONES.

Platinum One of the noble metals. See MORE ABOUT METALS.

Plique À Jour A kind of enameling. See MORE ABOUT METALS.

Point A measurement of weight for gemstones, especially diamonds. A point is a hundredth of a carat.

Potch A term used by Australian miners to describe opal with poor color or fire.

Precious Another one of those terms which sometimes means one thing, sometimes another. The *precious metals* are usually considered gold, silver, platinum and palladium, as distinguished from the *base metals* (all others). *Precious stones* usually refers to diamonds, sapphires, rubies and emeralds, although in the term *precious topaz* what is meant is that the stone is *real* topaz, not citrine (yellow quartz), which resembles it. Ask questions!

Profile Cut A modern variation of the brilliant cut, making very economical use of the diamond material. Also called *princess cut*.

Pyrope Red garnet. See SEMIPRECIOUS STONES.

Quartz The most common mineral, quartz or silicon oxide takes many forms and many colors. As crystals it is the material for the gemstones amethyst (purple), citrine (yellow), smoky quartz (gray brown) and rock crystal (clear).

In its massy, noncrystalline form it provides all the various agates and chalcedonies. Pulverized into tiniest bits, it is the material of sand; and heated and fused, it is glass.

Red Gold An alloy of gold with copper, or copper and silver. It is also called *pink gold*.

Repoussé A method of working or decorating metal by using a hammer and punches to model it up from the back (the opposite of *chasing*). This is an ancient technique, as chasing is, and examples of magnificent repoussé work by Greek craftsmen adorn our museums. Later, during the Renaissance, the goldsmiths excelled

181

at this kind of work, and today it is still an important technique for decorating gold and silver.

Rhinestone Usually a cheap glass stone, imitating a diamond.

Rhodium Plating Sometimes used on silver, rhodium plating gives the usually soft, mellow metal a hard, shiny surface that many people—including myself—find unattractive. However, rhodium plating is very durable, and it makes silver tarnish-free. It is a platinumlike metal, harder, whiter and shinier than platinum.

Rhodonite A pink stone which is used for beads and inexpensive jewelry, and looks rather like pink marble.

Ring Guard A thin metal band which, when attached to the inside of a too-large ring, improves its fit. Ring guards were once made of gold, but are now usually made of baser metal. If you use a ring guard on a soft, high-karat gold ring shank, be careful that it doesn't move around and scratch the finish of the gold.

Ring Gauge This is an instrument which measures the size of the ring you need. One system is to have a kind of key ring with various metal rings on it. By trying these on you can determine your own size. Another popular gauge is a *mandrel*—a long, conical rod marked with ring sizes. If you slip a ring over this mandrel, it will come to rest on the mark that tells what size it is.

Ripe Pearl One with a fine sheen, or *orient*.

River Pearl Freshwater pearl. See PEARLS.

Rolled Gold A kind of heavy gold plating in which a layer of base metal, often brass, is sandwiched in between two layers of gold.

Rondelle A thin spacer bead strung between important gemstone or metal beads, usually in the shape of a disc with faceted edges.

Rose Cut An old-fashioned diamond cut, nowadays seen almost exclusively in antique jewelry. Old "roses," as diamonds cut this way are fondly called, have a grayish look because they are simply faceted and don't refract as much fiery light as more elaborately cut stones. The rose cut is domed on top and flattish on the bottom. Diamonds cut this way are not as valuable (in dollars and cents) as brilliant cuts, but they have a charm all their own, and are eagerly collected and lovingly worn.

Rosé Refers to the delicate blush of pink in fine pearls. See PEARLS.

Rouge Jeweler's rouge, or polishing rouge, is soft red iron oxide, sometimes impregnated into a cloth, which jewelers use for surface polishing of metals and gemstones.

Ruby The precious, rare, clear red crystal corundum. Its best color is described as *pigeon's blood*.
See THE PRECIOUS STONES: RUBIES AND SAPPHIRES.

Sapphire The other colors of the clear, gemstone-quality corundum, exclusive of red (which is called *ruby*). Sapphires come in yellow, pink, white, violet, green and all shades of blue, but the most preferred color—the one most associated with the word "sapphire"—is soft velvety cornflower blue.
See THE PRECIOUS STONES: RUBIES AND SAPPHIRES.

Sardonyx Reddish brown chalcedony with bands of lighter and darker color, sometimes used for cameos or seals.

Schiller A German word meaning iridescence or glitter, sometimes used to describe the adularescence of a moonstone, or the play of light from within in any gemstone.

Seed Pearls Tiny pearls each weighing less than one quarter of a grain.

Shoulders Just as shoulders are on both sides of your head, this is that part of a ring shank on both sides of the center stone.

Silver The most common precious metal.
For more details, see the chapter on SILVER.

Sodalite A royal blue stone, sometimes mistaken for lapis lazuli.
See SEMIPRECIOUS STONES.

Solder Metal used in liquid form to cement two metal surfaces. The solder is heated until it runs, then set in place and allowed to cool. With it, a *flux* is used to clean the metal surfaces and encourage the solder to flow.

The proper soldering of any piece of jewelry is with self-metal; that is, gold on gold, silver on silver, etc. To use a solder that is softer than the metal joined is to risk a poor seam. Lead solder, which is extremely soft and weak and has the deadly quality of eating into gold if used on it, is to be avoided at all costs. Lead soldering is the telltale sign of a cheap job, a careless workman and a flawed piece.

Solitaire A fine stone, usually a diamond, set alone.

Soudé A composite stone. Another name for this is *triplet* (if three pieces are used) or *doublet* (if two). A soudé stone is a fake, and to be avoided, for its real purpose is to make you believe that the "sandwich" is one perfect gemstone.

Spinel A magnesium-aluminum oxide as hard as topaz. When it is transparent and occurs in a bright red color, it is often mistaken for ruby. See SEMIPRECIOUS STONES.

Sterling Silver of a fineness of 92.5 parts of pure silver to 7.5 of alloy, usually copper. See SILVER.

Table The large flat facet on the top of a gemstone.

Tanzanite Bluish violet gemstone discovered in 1967 in Tanzania. See SEMIPRECIOUS STONES.

Tiffany & Co. Probably the most famous jewelry store in the world. Founded by Charles Tiffany in 1837, the store has consistently been famous for the high quality of its gemstones, as well as its patrons. At Fifth Avenue and Fifty-seventh Street, it commands one of the prime corners in New York City. The store is responsible for the marketing of work by many famous designers such as Jean Schlumberger, Angela Cummings, Elsa Peretti and Paloma Picasso. No Tiffany salesman will sell a man a diamond ring; Tiffany's doesn't think it's appropriate. Louis Comfort Tiffany, Charles's son, was the artist in glass who was responsible for Tiffany glass and Tiffany lamps, which now sell for astronomical prices—if available. The Tiffany setting, a plain pronged setting for a solitaire diamond, is the favorite for most engagement rings, and is almost as famous as the store itself.

Tiger's Eye Chatoyant golden brown quartz. See SEMI-PRECIOUS STONES.

Topaz Topaz is not always warm sherry brown, though that is the most favored color. It also comes in yellow, pink, blue, greenish blue and, most commonly, colorless. See SEMIPRECIOUS STONES.

Touchstone The "stone" or dense ceramic on which a metal is rubbed to be tested. For more details, see GOLD.

Tourmaline While most people think of dark green or bright pink, my favorite color of tourmaline is a combination of both: green shading into pink and called, appropriately, *watermelon tourmaline*. For more details, see the chapter on SEMIPRECIOUS STONES.

Tumbling A method of grinding and polishing semiprecious stones by rubbing one against the other in a closed container, keeping them in continuous motion, all in the presence of water and polishing grit.

The polished stones produced are called *baroques*, which means they are uneven in shape. Usually this is done with the various massy quartz stones, but theoretically any materials of equivalent hardness could be tumbled to a polish. I have seen tumbled garnets and amethysts from India, as well as other tumbled gemstones, but for the more precious stones, too much is lost (and risked) in tumbling.

Turquoise A soft blue stone that is the "sky stone" of the

American Indians and the favored stone for most Indian jewelry. For more details, see SEMIPRECIOUS STONES.

Vermeil Usually used to mean silver overlaid with gold.

Wedding Ring If you have read the entry on engagement rings, you know that wedding rings developed from betrothal rings. Early Christians took the marriage vows and gave a ring; this was about the time, too, when the third finger of the left hand was chosen to receive it. The ancient Romans believed that a vein from that finger, the *vena amoris*, went straight to the heart.

Early wedding rings had symbolic motifs, such as hearts, hands and knots or sentimental inscriptions, and many had gems as well. The "plain gold band" did not become standard till later. In medieval times the left hand was changed to the right—no one quite knows why—and wedding rings, though placed on this finger during the ceremony, were actually worn on the thumb.

By 1549 the Book of Common Prayer again decreed that the third finger of the left hand was the correct one for the wedding ring, but thumb-wearing persisted. The Puritans tried to abolish ring wearing as frivolous, but the wedding ring prevailed, and by the nineteenth century it was customary to buy a separate ring for an engagement symbol, and a plain gold band for marriage. A century earlier Dr. Johnson defined a ring as "a circular instrument placed upon the noses of hogs and the fingers of women to restrain them and bring them into subjugation." In fact, men have worn wedding rings too—more often in Europe than in America—but the custom is growing. In Eastern Orthodox ceremonies the bride and groom both wear a ring, the groom of silver, the lucky bride of gold.

Wisconsin Pearls Freshwater pearls, from Wisconsin or elsewhere.

Yu Chinese name for *jadeite*.

Zircon A stone that comes in many colors and is almost as fiery as a diamond. Colorless zircons are often mistaken for the harder stone. See SEMIPRECIOUS STONES.